BOOT CAMP

Equipping Men with
Integrity for Spiritual Warfare

Jason Hardin

Boot Camp: Equipping Men with Integrity for Spiritual Warfare
© 2009 by DeWard Publishing Company, Ltd.
P.O. Box 6259, Chillicothe, Ohio 45601
800.300.9778
www.dewardpublishing.com

Unless otherwise noted, all Scripture quotations are from The Holy Bible, English Standard Version®, copyright © 2001 by Crossway Bibles, a publishing ministry of Good News Publishers. Used by permission. All rights reserved. Any emphasis to scripture quotations is added.

"Still the Cause Before Us" © 2002 by M.W. Bassford is used with permission. "The Army of Our Lord" © 1994 by Richard and Anne Morrison is used with permission.

Cover design by Jonathan Hardin.

Reasonable care has been taken to trace original sources for any excerpts and quotations appearing in this book and to document such information in the footnotes. For material not the public domain, fair-use standards and practices were followed. Should any attribution be found to be incorrect or incomplete, the publisher welcomes written documentation supporting correction for subsequent printings.

Printed in the United States of America.

ISBN: 978-0-9798893-7-0

For Shelly

Who, with the imperishable beauty of her gentle and quiet spirit, inspires me each day to be the man of integrity she deserves.

Contents

Part Three: The Lord's Armory

Conclusion: Our Battle Cry

Preface

Now to Him who is able to do far more abundantly beyond all
that we ask or think, according to the power that works within
us, to Him be the glory in the church and in Christ Jesus to all
generations forever and ever. Amen. (Eph 3.20–21, NASB)

There is a rock that has a special place on my desk. A single word
is engraved on its face: **IMAGINE**.

The world of men has been shaped by the power of imagination. Timeless myths of extraordinary valor are handed down
from generation to generation. Little boys spend ordinary after-
noons pretending to be medieval crusaders who fight for the worthiest of causes. The athlete relentlessly trains with visions of a
gold medal hanging around his neck. The artist dreams of his
crowning masterpiece. The astronaut straps himself inside of a
rocket pointed for the stars. Why? George Bernard Shaw offered
a theory when he wrote, "Some men see things as they are and ask
why. Others dream of things that never were and ask why not."[1]

Our God-given ability to imagine allows us to dream of what
could be. It challenges us to see what should be. An unquenchable
thirst drives us—in varying aspects of life—to go beyond the ordinary and to reach for the incredible. What we don't always appreciate, however, is that there is no more vital arena wherein such
determination is needed than the life of the disciple of Christ.

"So God created man in his own image, in the image of God
he created him" (Gen 1.27). Despite the countless physical characteristics that distinguish human beings from each other, we are
each image-bearers. The Creator of the universe "has put eternity

into man's heart" (Ecc 3.11), blessing us with the capacity to yearn for something more. He is described in his revelation to mankind as the One who is able to do far more abundantly beyond all that we ask or think, and he beckons us to join him in a quest of magnificent proportions.

Men love the epic tales of warriors who have defied the odds, proven to be larger-than-life at the decisive moment and led other men in efforts that have shaped the course of history. From the *Iliad* and the *Odyssey* to the latest Hollywood hero who single-handedly saves the world, men seem naturally to imagine being "that kind" of man.

But there is a greater story. There is a grander adventure. It is a divine chronicle of eternal magnitude in which you, in one way or another, will play your own unique part. Our Father in heaven yearns to awaken the awareness within each human being that there is no epic more awesome than that of Immanuel, God with us. He is the Son of the Source. He has provided the perfect pattern for true manhood. He has furnished the means of shaping, not just our imaginations, but our very lives into harmony with the glory of our Creator. And he invites you to join his ranks.

That's what this book, and the entire IMAGE project, is all about.

Imagine Man As God Envisioned

You hold in your hands the first of five volumes in the IMAGE series of books for men. A journey of sorts begins on the pages that follow wherein we are each encouraged to imagine living as our Father has always intended. We begin with the letter **I**, which will stand throughout the series for the foundational principle of *integrity*. Remove integrity from mankind's relationship with God and all that is left is an empty shell of selfishness and despair. That said, I hope it is abundantly clear that our ultimate goal is to mature beyond simply imagining what our Creator has envisioned to enlisting and thriving as loyal soldiers of the cross.

A vivid template of spiritual warfare permeates the New Testament Scriptures and such will be our framework in this series.

This first volume is set in the context of a spiritual "Boot Camp" experience. Just as the soldier who lives to fight another day learns the basics in Boot Camp, so the soldier of the cross must begin with the cornerstone of integrity.

Lastly, it must be noted that I am no expert. I'm an ordinary guy whose only qualifications for writing this series are a passion for the Savior and an earnest desire to encourage my fellow soldiers on the battlefield. The challenge of writing this series pales in comparison with the task of practicing what I've preached. I continue to foolishly stumble at times, disappointing my Master and the people around me. But I have also tasted and trust in "the immeasurable greatness of his power toward us who believe" (Eph 1.19). My prayer is that this work will be one more signpost pointing in the right direction on our long journey home.

May the everlasting God be gracious to us and daring in his use of us as we grow in our efforts "to be conformed to the image of his Son" (Rom 8.29).

To him be the glory.

Jason Hardin

Let all who stand with Christ the Lord:
Each good and faithful servant,
Take up the shield and bear the sword,
With heart and spirit fervent.
Behind the Rock of Ages,
And armed with holy pages,
If God be for us, who can fear?
O let us be courageous!

The early saints held fast indeed,
And One would soon reward them;
For mounted on His battle steed,
"The Word of God" came toward them.
And through the slaughter glorious,
His army rode victorious!
Their cause, now aged two thousand years,
Is still the cause before us.

Almighty God, whose outstretched arm
Is certain to defend us,
We pray, where'er the present harm,
"Into the conflict, send us!"
By calling and election,
With power and protection,
Our cross of duty leads from here
To crowns of resurrection.

O God, we know by pressing on,
A field is ever nearing;
Where all our mortal strength is gone,
We lie down in the clearing.
Should nightfall overtake us,
The morning hymn will wake us!
And when our Life and Light appears,
Immortal Father, take us.

"Still The Cause Before Us," C.A. Roberts

Introduction

Picture it in your mind. The epic battle scene. How many of the movies that men love have portrayed it in one way or another? A general-turned-slave-turned-gladiator fights for honor and justice in the ancient Colosseum of Rome. A struggle against all odds is waged on the fields of Middle Earth while the smallest of heroes carries the heaviest of burdens to the slopes of Mount Doom. A bold Scotsman uses the steel of his blade and the fire of his intellect to rally his countrymen to liberation. A down-on-his-luck farmboy finds his place in the fight against the Dark Side amidst the stars of a galaxy far, far away.

Regardless of the setting, inspiring warriors who stood their ground in larger-than-life conflicts have stirred the hearts and imaginations of men for generations. What would it be like to courageously lead a band of brothers into a battle of critical importance? How would it feel to actually hunker down in the trenches and help to turn the tide of a war? What would it mean to follow one of the world's great leaders to the end?

We stand at the trail head of our own epic journey. With the same mental effort you use to envision the gladiator in the Colosseum or the hobbit in the Shire, with the same imagination you use to picture the medieval warrior wielding his sword or the X-Wing pilot soaring beyond the clouds, picture the following scene in your mind.

> I saw heaven opened, and behold a white horse! The one sitting on it is called Faithful and True, and in righteousness he judges and makes war. His eyes are like a flame of fire, and on his head

are many diadems, and he has a name written that no one knows but himself. He is clothed in a robe dipped in blood, and the name by which he is called is The Word of God. And the armies of heaven, arrayed in fine linen, white and pure, were following him on white horses. From his mouth comes a sharp sword with which to strike down the nations, and he will rule them with a rod of iron. He will tread the winepress of the fury of the wrath of God the Almighty. On his robe and on his thigh he has a name written, King of kings and Lord of lords.

Then I saw an angel standing in the sun, and with a loud voice he called to all the birds that fly directly overhead, "Come, gather for the great supper of God, to eat the flesh of kings, the flesh of captains, the flesh of mighty men, the flesh of horses and their riders, and the flesh of all men, both free and slave, both small and great." And I saw the beast and the kings of the earth with their armies gathered to make war against him who was sitting on the horse and against his army. (Rev 19.11–19)

Grasp this point: you were born into a world at war. It is a war that has been raging for thousands of years. It has little to do with high-tech fighter planes, tanks or rocket launchers. It isn't centered in one part of the globe. It's all around you. As you read this book. As you eat your dinner. As you drive to work. As you spend your money. As you surf the Internet. As you relax with friends and family. As you worship. As you watch television. As you wake up. As you go to sleep.

You cannot escape this war because you are its prize. It is being waged over your soul and the souls of those you love. You cannot walk away from it, never to be involved in the conflict. It is happening all the time, in every corner of Creation. You can wish that you never knew, that you were blissfully unaware of the whole thing, but such will make little difference. Feigning ignorance only leads you directly into the Enemy's trap. The war has come to you.

In the cinematic version of *The Lord Of The Rings: The Two Towers*, King Théoden sits on his throne as he is warned by multiple messengers of the evil growing on all fronts. Innocent villagers have had no warning of the coming destruction. Vicious enemies are freely roaming the land, burning as they go, and all that has happened thus far seems only to be a foretaste of the terror that will soon be unleashed. The longer he delays, the deeper he and his people fall into the cleverly laid trap. But there are those who would come to his aid if only Théoden were to ask. He is counseled to ride out and meet the Enemy head on. "Draw him away from your women and children," Gandalf encourages. "You must fight." Still, the King resists: "I know what it is you want of me, but I will not bring further death to my people. I will not risk open war." The point is finally driven home by Aragorn: "Open war is upon you, whether you would risk it or not."

So also with you. Truly, the only thing necessary for the triumph of evil is for good men to do nothing. The problem, as aptly described by John Eldredge, is that "too many Christians have approached their lives as though they were stepping onto the beaches of Normandy on D-Day with a lawn chair and a book to read." [1]

The vivid language of Revelation 19 seeks to impress upon us the seriousness of the struggle. Immerse yourself in the intense and graphic imagery. A white horse draws near with a mighty rider bearing multiple titles: Faithful and True, the Word of God, King of all kings and Lord of all lords. His declared purpose is to judge and make war. His eyes are like a flame of fire and a sharp sword comes out of his mouth. He wears not one, but several crowns of royalty. His robe is soaked with blood—proof of the cost that comes with the conflict. But he is not alone. Angelic soldiers arrayed in dazzling white linen faithfully follow him on battle steeds of their own. The rider brings with him the raging wrath of Almighty God. And on the opposite side, a great beast and the kings and armies of the earth gather for war. The glories of heaven and the horrors of hell are about to be unleashed upon one another.

God's Spirit used such graphic language to make an impression on the minds of men. Light and darkness, good and evil, purity and perversion are locked in a terrible state of conflict, and you and I cannot afford to ignore it. Paul drew back the curtains of the eternal and described it as a struggle "against the rulers, against the powers, against the world forces of this darkness, against the spiritual forces of wickedness in the heavenly places" (Eph 6.12, NASB).

How ironic, then, that we already know how this greatest of stories will end. While the great wars of history have required years to fight and volumes to describe, the details of the outcome of this conflict are few and concise. In the end, it will be no contest. The victory of the Word of God has already been declared as certain.

Armed with that assurance, the revelation to John presents us with a basic premise and a choice. Though the forces of evil are powerful, they cannot defeat the will of the Creator. With allegiance to the Christ comes absolute victory; loyalty to the Enemy brings certain destruction. The outcome of the war has already been decided.

Nevertheless, individual battles continue to this day. We discover in another vivid scene from Revelation:

> Now war arose in heaven, Michael and his angels fighting against the dragon. And the dragon and his angels fought back, but he was defeated and there was no longer any place for them in heaven. And the great dragon was thrown down, that ancient serpent, who is called the devil and Satan, the deceiver of the whole world—he was thrown down to the earth, and his angels were thrown down with him. (Rev 12.7–9)

In a world overcome with sin and rebellion, a cross was raised that judged the darkness and banished its prince. A triumphant shout was heard in heaven: "Now the salvation and the power and the kingdom of our God and the authority of his Christ have come, for the accuser of our brothers has been thrown down, who accuses them day and night before our God" (Rev 12.10).

No matter what he does, the Enemy simply cannot displace the Creator as Supreme. As the great dragon appears to have won his decisive victory, the astonishing plan of the Father is fulfilled. The victory of Jesus is sealed through shameful death and triumphant resurrection. God has conquered in the most unlikely of ways.

But before the scene is left, a warning is clearly given. "Then the dragon became furious … and went off to make war … on those who keep the commandments of God and hold to the testimony of Jesus" (Rev 12.17). In other words, the war has come to our own backyard.

As Robert Harkrider summarizes in his commentary on Revelation:

> The proud, arrogant armies of the beast are now brought to nothing. The kingdom of God which Rome attempted to stamp out still stands. This particular battle of Armageddon was fought centuries ago. The Roman Empire backing the pagan god-Caesar worship was destroyed, thus the persecuting force against the church was brought down.
>
> In principle, other "Armageddons" have taken place and perhaps shall yet be in the future because Satan continues to wage battle against the purpose of God. Satan did not cease to exist, and he has employed other methods to fight against the kingdom of God on earth. [2]

Make no mistake about it. As long as this earth stands, the victory of the Christ is certain, but the war rages on. As a seasoned veteran of the struggle, Peter warned his fellow soldiers,

> Be sober-minded; be watchful. Your adversary the devil prowls around like a roaring lion, seeking someone to devour. Resist him, firm in your faith, knowing that the same kinds of suffering are being experienced by your brotherhood throughout the world. (1 Pet 5.8–9)

As long as there are souls in the balance, Satan will tirelessly seek to draw God's children away from their place in the promised triumph. In the meantime, we are left with a choice. On which side will we fight? Which outcome will ultimately be our own?

The pathway of the conqueror has already been defined by the King of kings and His mighty men of the past. The Holy Spirit tells us that the secrets of victory are based upon firmness of faith and a resilient willingness to enlist in something eternally larger than ourselves. The invitation remains open. Paul described the glorious cause in Ephesians 3.8–12:

> To me, though I am the very least of all the saints, this grace was given, to preach to the Gentiles the unsearchable riches of Christ, and to bring to light for everyone what is the plan of the mystery hidden for ages in God who created all things, so that through the church the manifold wisdom of God might now be made known to the rulers and authorities in the heavenly places. This was according to the eternal purpose that he has realized in Christ Jesus our Lord, in whom we have boldness and access with confidence through our faith in him.

As a 21st century soldier of the cross, you are but one piece of the eternal puzzle for victory. "The plan of the mystery" is much larger than any of us. But who among us knows what pivotal part in the conflict we could play? "Who knows whether you have not come to the kingdom for such a time as this?" (Est 4.14).

The trumpet call for warriors of integrity is ringing. How will you respond? You can stubbornly continue to ignore the signs all around you. You can helplessly cower in shame and fear. By your unwillingness to do anything, you can remain enslaved in the Enemy's ranks. Or you can boldly draw the line in the sand, standing with confidence through your faith in the Lord of hosts and reply, "Master, here am I."

Regardless of your choice, open war is upon you—whether you would risk it or not.

Part One

The Beginning of Our Journey

For God, who said, "Let light shine out of darkness," has shone in our hearts to give the light of the knowledge of the glory of God in the face of Jesus Christ.

2 Corinthians 4.6

1

Boot Camp

Face to Face with the One Who Sees Your Potential

And I said: "Woe is me! For I am lost; for I am a man of unclean lips, and I dwell in the midst of a people of unclean lips; for my eyes have seen the King, the LORD of hosts!" (Isa 6.5)

Boot Camp. Where a soldier learns the basics. Where he is equipped for the battles ahead. Boot Camp is where he tests his weapons and learns to fight with discipline and honor. Boot Camp is where careful, deliberate time is taken to learn from the veterans of previous wars. What obstacles confronted them? Where did they meet the enemy? Most importantly, how did they succeed?

The book you hold in your hands is the equivalent of Boot Camp in the IMAGE series of books for men. It is here that we will begin to discover—or rediscover—the character and qualities our Creator expects his image-bearers to exhibit.

Initiation

Imagine. What would it be like to enter the Boot Camp of the King of kings? Mentally place yourself in that scenario. As you approach the entrance, the very first thing you notice are words engraved by the finger of God that will outlast the strongest marble: "Therefore, since we are surrounded by so great a cloud of witnesses, let us also lay aside every weight, and sin which clings so closely, and let us run with endurance the race that is set before us" (Heb 12.1).

Upon your arrival, you are led with the other recruits into an ancient colosseum. Its walls are more massive than any structure mankind could dream of building. Its symmetry is perfect. Its grandeur, breathtaking. As you prepare yourself deep inside its bowels, you hear the rumble. The crescendo of the crowd's cheer echoes from above. The whole structure quakes with the shouts.

As you make your way up the steps and into the dusty arena, you are exhilarated beyond description. The brilliance of the light above nearly blinds you as you clear the entrance. And then it hits you. The roar of the assembly. Without even thinking, you are irresistibly compelled to look around. You can't help but turn in a couple of circles as you struggle to take in the grandness of the scene around you. The clamor is deafening.

Within the crowd, near the front row, you see Moses. Beside him is Gideon. In the adjacent section you spot David. Across the way, there is Elijah. As you get a brief glimpse of their faces between the raised hands, your mind quite naturally fills to the brim with those ancient accounts. You envision Sinai wrapped in smoke because Jehovah has descended upon it in fire. You recall the story of a pitifully small band of soldiers who armed themselves with nothing more than torches and empty pots. You call to mind the simple shepherd boy who defied an armored giant. You marvel at the seasoned prophet who confidently called down fire from heaven. Truly, this is a "great cloud of witnesses" unlike anything you could ever imagine. And you suddenly realize that they are cheering for you.

Your mind is irresistibly flooded with questions, but just as you get your bearings, the drums begin to beat, the trumpets make their clarion call, and all rise to look in the same direction. An excited hush falls over the entire assembly. Beyond the crowd of glorified mortals you discern a heavenly parade made up of millions upon millions of armored angels with wings rising and falling in unison. They march in perfect cadence to the reverent phrase,

"Holy, holy, holy," with the banners of the kingdom of God flying high overhead.

Suddenly, the great host comes to a perfect and simultaneous stop. They turn and cry out as one with a loud and perfect roar: "Worthy is the Lamb who was slain, to receive power and wealth and wisdom and might and honor and glory and blessing! To him who sits on the throne and to the Lamb be blessing and honor and glory and might forever and ever" (Rev 5.12–13).

And there he is. A long robe and a golden sash are wrapped around his chest. His hair is white like wool, as white as snow. His eyes shine like flames of fire. His feet glow as bronze just removed from a furnace. His voice thunders like the mightiest of waterfalls. He holds seven stars in his right hand. A sharp two-edged sword comes out of his mouth. His face is as bright as the sun on the most brilliantly cloudless day.

In your mind, come face to shining face with your King in Boot Camp and beyond. More than ever before, appreciate Jesus as "the founder and perfecter of our faith, who for the joy that was set before him endured the cross, despising the shame, and is seated at the right hand of the throne of God" (Heb 12.2).

As the eyes that can burn the impurities right out of your life come to rest upon you, you realize more than ever before that you are not your own. You are standing before the most authoritative figure in history. You have hope because the price you could not afford to pay was underwritten with the blood of the slain Lamb of God. Yet, you are more painfully aware than ever before of your unworthiness and foolish insubordination. You know all too well why Isaiah exclaimed "Woe is me! For I am lost" (Isa 6.5). You have seen the King of glory with your own eyes and your sense of awe mixed with shame and fear is suffocating. So you do the only thing you can, falling on your face to the ground.

With hands trembling and eyes locked on nothing but the grainy sand of the arena, you suddenly feel his hand on your shoulder. His words of reassurance speak to the deepest part of your being. "Don't be afraid! I am the First and the Last. I am the living one who died. Look, I am alive forever and ever! And

I hold the keys of death and the grave" (Rev 1.17–18, NLT). He welcomes you to the arena and rejoices with the angels of heaven at your willingness to enter the kingdom of light. You are to be commended for entering the battle for your soul and the souls of those you love. He assures you, however, that you have a long way to go. The journey has only begun.

As he looks at you, you feel utterly exposed. There is nothing hidden from his gaze. He sees what forbidden paths you have traveled. He knows the selfish work of your careless and unrighteous hands. He pierces through those wandering eyes right into your mind. He easily finds the darkest corners you have kept successfully locked away from everyone. Everyone but him.

He sees each of your flaws, but he also acknowledges your humble and penitent heart. He feels your godly sorrow. He knows your touch of faith and he recognizes his own blood that has washed your garments clean so that you might gain access to this arena. You have a long way to go, but he sees your potential.

He is the same Jesus who walked the shores of the Sea of Galilee and called to common fishermen, "Follow me, and I will make you fishers of men" (Matt 4.18–19). He is the same Teacher who passed by Matthew sitting in the tax booth and said, "Follow me" (Matt 9.9). He is the same Savior who warned Peter that Satan desired to "sift" him "like wheat" (Luke 22.31) and graciously restored him after his denial (John 21.15–19).

What is it that Jesus saw in Andrew, James and John more than the other fishermen of Galilee? Why Matthew in the middle of a city full of tax collectors? What set Peter apart from Judas? What did Jesus find in Nicodemus and the woman at Jacob's well that was left untapped by the rich young ruler and so many of the Pharisees?

Potential. A simple willingness to leave behind what was weighing them down. A yielding response to his invitation, regardless of the cost. A concerted effort to go all the way for him.

Realize that just as he saw their potential, he sees yours. The only question is, how will you wield that potential?

The Tragedy of Wasted Potential

How many eager young men have taken life-long dreams to places like West Point or Annapolis only to have them dashed for lack of personal discipline? They may have had family heritage, physical stature and past intellectual achievements lauding their praise prior to their arrival, but lost sight of the goal. They took their eyes off of the finish line. They learned the hard way that childhood dreams can vanish in an instant of recklessness.

Conversely, how many "long shots" have gone to such academies unarmed with a father's reputation, in great need of physical exercise, and destined to flunk without a tutor? And yet, in spite of the obvious obstacles, how many of those long shots have evolved into men who grew to greatness with discipline, correction and training to reach their fullest potential and ultimately alter the course of the world?

On April 23, 1910, in a speech at the Sorbonne in Paris, Theodore Roosevelt said:

> It is not the critic who counts: not the man who points out how the strong man stumbles or where the doer of deeds could have done better. The credit belongs to the man who is actually in the arena, whose face is marred by dust and sweat and blood, who strives valiantly, who errs and comes up short again and again, because there is no effort without error or shortcoming, but who knows the great enthusiasms, the great devotions, who spends himself for a worthy cause; who, at the best, knows, in the end, the triumph of high achievement, and who, at the worst, if he fails, at least he fails while daring greatly, so that his place shall never be with those cold and timid souls who knew neither victory nor defeat. [1]

Our King has spent time in the arena. He knows what it's like to have his face marred by the dust of the wilderness. He bears the scars that prove his loyalty. This greatest of warriors rescued his people with his own tears, sweat and blood from the kingdom of darkness. And now he looks to you. He invites you to leave behind the ranks of those cold, timid souls who avoid the conflict at all costs.

You probably remember the old Army slogan, "Be all you can be." Spiritually speaking, you may feel that such is a beautiful ideal, but largely unattainable. "I'm too busy." "I've wasted too much time already." "I've made too many mistakes." "I don't have what it takes." If that's you, remember who is in the stands, cheering you on.

Moses

Recall eighty-year-old Moses, full of excuses. God knows his past. He has seen the mistakes. He has watched as the former-prince-of-Egypt-turned-obscure-shepherd lived in exile for forty years in the wilderness of Midian. Still, he sees potential.

> "I am the God of your father, the God of Abraham, the God of Isaac, and the God of Jacob. …I have surely seen the affliction of my people who are in Egypt and have heard their cry because of their taskmasters. I know their sufferings, and I have come down to deliver them out of the hand of the Egyptians. …Come, I will send you to Pharaoh that you may bring my people, the children of Israel, out of Egypt." (Exod 3.6–10)

Beyond the excuses is an answer. Behind the inadequacies is a leader. On the far side of fear is a warrior who, with a spokesman, a rod, and the help of the great I AM will deliver millions of Abraham's descendants to freedom.

Gideon

Remember Gideon. Picture him in your mind. He is hiding. For seven years the Midianites have oppressed his people. The men of Israel, who had made the hearts of the surrounding nations "melt" in the days of Joshua (Josh 2.11) now hide themselves in dens and caves of the mountains. As numerous as the locusts, the Midianites and their camels have been routinely raiding Gideon's people and their crops.

In Judges 6 we find Gideon threshing his wheat in a winepress. Don't just read over that. Remember what a winepress is for. It has nothing to do with the threshing of wheat and everything to do with grapes! But here is Gideon—hunkered down, working quietly and quickly in an effort to hide himself and his harvest prize.

And yet, while Gideon may hide for a time from the Midianites, he cannot hide from his Maker. "The angel of the LORD appeared to him and said to him, 'The LORD is with you, O mighty man of valor'" (Jdg 6.12). Read that again, pausing to appreciate this ironic description. "Man of valor"? Men of valor don't routinely hide from the enemy. Gideon certainly doesn't look the part. By his own confession, "My clan is the weakest in Manasseh, and I am the least in my father's house" (Jdg 6.15). But what does God see in this man who has to hide while preparing his wheat? Potential. "I will be with you, and you shall strike the Midianites as one man" (Jdg 6.16).

Beyond the excuses is an answer. Behind the inadequacies is a leader. On the far side of fear is a warrior who, with a wet fleece as a sign, 300 men, and some empty jars will slay 120,000 Midianites.

David

Recall young David. He is the youngest of eight sons. While his three oldest brothers have followed King Saul to war against the Philistines, David feeds his father's sheep. He has no military experience, no moments in the national spotlight, just long days and lonely nights on the hills outside of Bethlehem. When we are first introduced to David, he is largely a nobody. He is easily forgotten and often dismissed.

But Jehovah comes with a message: "Do not look on his appearance or on the height of his stature. ...For the LORD sees not as man sees: man looks on the outward appearance, but the LORD looks on the heart" (1 Sam 16.7). What does God see in young David that sets him apart from his battle-seasoned brothers? What does the Creator notice that even David's own father may have overlooked? Potential. "Arise, anoint him," Jehovah tells the prophet Samuel. "For this is he" (1 Sam 16.12).

Saul, "greatly afraid," hides in his tent. David's brothers ridicule the fact that the runt of the family has even come to the battlefield. But David is the only man—young or old—who approaches Goliath.

Beyond the excuses is an answer. Behind the inadequacies is a leader. On the far side of fear is a warrior who, with a shepherd's sling, five smooth stones, and an unshakeable faith in the God of the armies of Israel will conquer a giant.

Elijah

Remember the great prophet Elijah. He acts as God's spokesman during the reign of King Ahab, who is described as doing "evil in the sight of the LORD, more than all who were before him" (1 Kgs 16.30). That's saying something when we remember that Ahab reigns after a bunch of brazen idolaters, drunks and murderers. But it's precisely at this point in history that Elijah the Tishbite steps into the public eye. He doesn't spread his message with a whisper. He doesn't hide in dark corners. He walks into the presence of the king himself and delivers the judgment of God: "As the LORD the God of Israel lives, before whom I stand, there shall be neither dew nor rain these years, except by my word" (1 Kgs 17.1).

Elijah's stand for Jehovah leads to a number of confrontations that eventually climax on Mount Carmel. "How long will you go limping between two different opinions?" Elijah challenges the people, "If the LORD is God, follow him; but if Baal, then follow him" (1 Kgs 18.21). In an effort to indisputably prove whom Israel owes its allegiance, Elijah proposes a showdown. The 450 prophets of Baal call upon their deity to answer and prove his worth. The grisly scene is summarized in 1 Kings 18.28–29: "They cried aloud and cut themselves after their custom with swords and lances, until the blood gushed out upon them. And as midday passed, they raved on until the time of the offering of the oblation, but there was no voice. No one answered; no one paid attention."

Elijah then calls upon "the God who answers by fire," and, "The fire of the LORD fell and consumed the burnt offering. The people fell on their faces and said, 'The LORD, he is God; the LORD, he is God'" (1 Kgs 18.38–39). The prophets of Baal are seized and subsequently slaughtered at the brook Kishon.

Mission accomplished, right? Surely now Elijah can relax. Not so fast. The queen herself "sent a messenger to Elijah, saying, 'So may the gods do to me and more also, if I do not make your life as the life of one of them by this time tomorrow'" (1 Kgs 19.1–2). And what is Elijah's reaction? "Then he was afraid, and he arose and ran for his life" (1 Kgs 19.3).

He goes a day's journey into the wilderness and finally settles under a broom tree. His plea is simple: "It is enough; now, O LORD, take away my life, for I am no better than my fathers" (1 Kgs 19.4). He has given up. Following his greatest triumph, he reasons from a mindset of discouragement and defeat.

But God isn't through with Elijah. After 40 long days and nights he confronts the prophet with a simple question: "What are you doing here, Elijah?" (1 Kgs 19.9). There is still work to be done. "Go," is Jehovah's commission. "Return on your way to the wilderness of Damascus" (1 Kgs 19.15). When he arrives, Elijah is charged with anointing new kings over God's people. Even after his crisis of faith, Elijah will stand as God's watchman over the descendants of Abraham for many more years.

What separates Elijah from Ahab? What fuels Elijah through these life-threatening events? Why doesn't God give up on him when he had obviously given up on himself? Elijah's Creator sees potential.

Beyond the excuses is an answer. Behind the inadequacies is a leader. On the far side of fear is a warrior who, with fearless courage, patient endurance, and a potent faith eventually leaves this life behind with chariots of fire and a whirlwind into heaven (2 Kgs 2).

Now It's up to You

These are just a few of the stories that could be drawn from this "great cloud of witnesses." Following the pattern drawn by the writer of Hebrews, time would fail to tell of Abel, Enoch, Noah, Abraham, Sarah, Joseph, Barak, Samson, Jephthah, Samuel and the prophets…

...who through faith conquered kingdoms, enforced justice, obtained promises, stopped the mouths of lions, quenched the power of fire, escaped the edge of the sword, were made strong out of weakness, became mighty in war, put foreign armies to flight. Women received back their dead by resurrection. Some were tortured, refusing to accept release, so that they might rise again to a better life. Others suffered mocking and flogging, and even chains and imprisonment. They were stoned, they were sawn in two, they were killed with the sword. They went about in skins of sheep and goats, destitute, afflicted, mistreated—of whom the world was not worthy—wandering about in deserts and mountains, and in dens and caves of the earth.

And all these, though commended through their faith, did not receive what was promised, since God had provided something better for us, that apart from us they should not be made perfect. (Heb 11.32–40)

Take the time to relish that truth. Be humbled by the inspired message. We stand in awe of these men, and rightfully so. Look at what they accomplished! Marvel at how far they pressed the battle. But recognize that you and I have the opportunity to be a part of something even "better."

These men served the purposes of God in their own generations and yet they could only fight for so long. Eventually their earthly strength failed and they went on to their reward. Their faith that forever impacted the struggle between good and evil has been immortalized in the Scriptures.

But who will rise up and fill that void now? The torch still burns brightly. To whom will it be passed? What troops will now fill the battlefield and claim what God has abundantly provided that is even "better"?

What about our situation could possibly be described as better? Consider Abraham, who by faith "obeyed when he was called to go out to a place that he was to receive as an inheritance. And he went out, not knowing where he was going" (Heb 11.8). As soldiers of the cross, our destination has been clearly defined.

Moses led millions of Israelites through a barren wilderness guided only by pillars of cloud and fire. Without those, he didn't know the way to freedom. On this side of the cross, the pathway is definitively marked for all.

"These all died in faith, not having received the things promised, but having seen them and greeted them from afar, and having acknowledged that they were strangers and exiles on the earth," they finished their spiritual journey victoriously (Heb 11.13). So many of those ancient warriors never received the things for which they hoped in this life. "All these, though commended through their faith, did not receive what was promised." Why? "Since God had provided something better for us, that apart from us they should not be made perfect" (Heb 11.39–40). The ancient heroes of the cross look to us to further the cause.

Let's listen as Peter drives the point home:

> In this you rejoice, though now for a little while, if necessary, you have been grieved by various trials, so that the tested genuineness of your faith—more precious than gold that perishes though it is tested by fire—may be found to result in praise and glory and honor at the revelation of Jesus Christ. Though you have not seen him, you love him. Though you do not now see him, you believe in him and rejoice with joy that is inexpressible and filled with glory, obtaining the outcome of your faith, the salvation of your souls.
>
> Concerning this salvation, the prophets who prophesied about the grace that was to be yours searched and inquired carefully, inquiring what person or time the Spirit of Christ in them was indicating when he predicted the sufferings of Christ and the subsequent glories. It was revealed to them that they were serving not themselves but you, in the things that have now been announced to you through those who preached the good news to you by the Holy Spirit sent from heaven, things into which angels long to look. (1 Pet 1.6–12)

Abraham, Moses, Gideon, Barak, Samson, Jephthah, David, Samuel and so many more like them pressed the battle front as far forward as they could. Now they look to you, to me, to all Christians to push it even further—perhaps even finishing the task in our own lifetime. Only God knows when the great conflict will come to its ultimate conclusion. Our task, and the task of each generation of God's people to come, is summarized in Hebrews 12.1–2:

> Therefore, since we are surrounded by so great a cloud of witnesses, let us also lay aside every weight, and sin which clings so closely, and let us run with endurance the race that is set before us, looking to Jesus, the founder and perfecter of faith, who for the joy that was set before him endured the cross, despising the shame, and is seated at the right hand of the throne of God.

As you gaze one more time around this great arena, you may feel unworthy. You may believe that everyone else could fight the fight and run the race but you. You may be afraid. You may have a mind filled with excuses.

Through the crowd, lock eyes with Moses. In the midst of the roar, discern the shouts of Gideon. In the sea of confusion, watch as David raises his hands. Amid the frenzy, recognize the confident smile of Elijah. Above it all, see the glorified Christ and know that one day, you can stand with them. One day, you can share your battle stories with all of the Lord's soldiers of all time. How? Why? Because your God sees your potential.

> In all these things we overwhelmingly conquer through Him who loved us. For I am convinced that neither death, nor life, nor angels, nor principalities, nor things present, nor things to come, nor powers, nor height, nor depth, nor any other created thing, will be able to separate us from the love of God, which is in Christ Jesus our Lord. (Rom 8.37–39, NASB)

"The Way of All the Earth"

As I wrote this chapter, an appropriate e-mail came across my desk. It was a son's poignant announcement of his own father's death.

> It is with natural sadness that I notify you of the death of my father…just nine days before his 98th birthday. But that sadness is mixed with pride, as at this time we are caused to remember the passing of a very capable soldier of the cross who devoted over 70 years to preaching the gospel and helping countless people learn the Truth.
>
> It's significant to note that even in great loss and several prob-

lems in recent times, he died with the Bible—his greatest possession—on his bedside table. The natural sadness is also mixed with relief as the problems that come with old age need no longer be endured.

Though we covet your prayers at this time, it is not entirely for our comfort in the loss. For our part, and given his age, we had expected it for several years. The greater tragedy being the loss to the world of his powerful influence.

Those of whom the world is not worthy. Those who abandon the excuses, grow beyond their inadequacies and conquer their fears. Those who courageously march behind their King and push the battle as far as they can. Such is the goal. Here is our finish line.

If you've seen the cinematic version of *The Lord Of The Rings: The Fellowship of the Ring*, you undoubtedly remember Frodo's dialogue with Gandalf as he contemplates the difficult road ahead.

Frodo: "I wish the Ring had never come to me. I wish none of this had happened."

Gandalf: "So do all who live to see such times. But that is not for them to decide. All we have to decide is what to do with the time that is given to us."

Welcome to Boot Camp. We've got a long way to go.

2

Currahee

The Mountain of God

It shall come to pass in the latter days that the mountain of the house of the LORD shall be established as the highest of the mountains, and shall be lifted up above the hills; and all the nations shall flow to it, and many peoples shall come, and say: "Come, let us go up to the mountain of the LORD, to the house of the God of Jacob, that he may teach us his ways and that we may walk in his paths." (Isa 2.2–3)

"Currahee!" That was the battle cry of some of the most courageous soldiers in the history of the United States—the Parachute Infantry Regiments of the 101st Airborne Division during World War II. While others shouted "Geronimo!" as they jumped from planes over the beaches of Normandy and beyond, this group and their rallying call were different. Unless you're familiar with the mountains of northern Georgia, however, you may have never even heard the word.

Currahee is the southernmost peak in the chain of the Blue Ridge Mountains. It's a Cherokee Indian word that means "stands alone," and the description is a perfect fit. From almost any road leading into Stephens County, Georgia, the 1,000 foot summit can be seen as it "stands alone" above the horizon.

During World War II, the mountain became a powerful symbol for the military. Currahee was selected as the site for the

Army's first Parachute Infantry Training Center, named Camp Toccoa after the nearby city. Runs up the slopes of Currahee were a painfully regular part of the regiment's training—three miles up, three miles down, nearly every day. The routine was arduous and demanding to say the least, but a motley group of young men from all over the country was slowly refined into one of America's most elite military regiments: the paratroopers. Wherever they went, whatever they faced, "Currahee!" was their rallying cry.

In an effort to find an inspiring call of our own as soldiers of the cross, let's turn our attention to a type of Currahee described by David in Psalm 24.

> The earth is the LORD's and the fullness thereof,
>   the world and those who dwell therein,
> for he has founded it upon the seas
>   and established it upon the rivers.
> Who shall ascend the hill of the LORD?
>   And who shall stand in his holy place?
> He who has clean hands and a pure heart,
>   who does not lift up his soul to what is false
>   and does not swear deceitfully.
> He will receive blessing from the LORD
>   and righteousness from the God of his salvation.
> Such is the generation of those who seek him,
>   who seek the face of the God of Jacob.
> Lift up your heads, O gates!
>   And be lifted up, O ancient doors,
>   that the King of glory may come in.
> Who is this King of glory?
>   The LORD, strong and mighty,
>   the LORD, mighty in battle!
> Lift up your heads, O gates!
>   And lift them up, O ancient doors,
>   that the King of glory may come in.
> Who is this King of glory?
>   The LORD of hosts,
>   he is the King of glory!

The earth is Jehovah's. How often we lose sight of that! It doesn't belong to us. We are simply stewards. Practically speaking, this means that every single thing around you—everything you "own," everything you like to think of as yours—belongs to God. Everything that fills the earth belongs to him, right along with every single person. After establishing that fundamental fact, David asks, "Who shall ascend the hill of the LORD? Who shall stand in His holy place?" Of all God's creatures, who may meet this challenge?

In search of an answer to that question, we return to Hebrews 12. After holding up Jesus as the supreme example of faith and pointing each disciple toward the ideal of endurance, the author of Hebrews also uses the analogy of a mountain.

> For you have not come to a mountain that can be touched and to a blazing fire, and to darkness and gloom and whirlwind, and to the blast of a trumpet and the sound of words which sound was such that those who heard begged that no further word be spoken to them. (Heb 12.18–19, NASB)

The first-century descendant of Abraham would have readily understood. The writer is recalling Mount Sinai as Israel congregated around its slopes and Jehovah descended from the heavens. "For they could not endure the order that was given, 'If even a beast touches the mountain, it shall be stoned.' Indeed, so terrifying was the sight that Moses said, 'I tremble with fear'" (Heb 12.20–21).

Follow the writer's train of thought as he moves from the historical footnote to a present-day exhortation. Each soldier of Christ must come face to face with a fact that is far more awe-inspiring than Old Testament Sinai.

> You have come to Mount Zion and to the city of the living God, the heavenly Jerusalem, and to innumerable angels in festal gathering, and to the assembly of the firstborn who are enrolled in heaven, and to God, the judge of all, and to the spirits of the righteous made perfect, and to Jesus, the mediator of a new covenant, and to the sprinkled blood that speaks a better word than the blood of Abel.

See that you do not refuse him who is speaking. For if they did not escape when they refused him who warned them on earth, much less will we escape if we reject him who warns from heaven. At that time his voice shook the earth, but now he has promised, "Yet once more I will shake not only the earth but also the heavens." This phrase, "Yet once more," indicates the removal of things that are shaken—that is, things that have been made—in order that the things that cannot be shaken may remain. Therefore let us be grateful for receiving a kingdom that cannot be shaken, and thus let us offer to God acceptable worship, with reverence and awe, for our God is a consuming fire. (Heb 12.22–29)

As Christians, we have come to Mount Zion. Here is our Currahee. Picture its majestic slopes in your mind.

The trail head is marked with a cross. From the outset you can't help but notice that the pathway has been stained with the blood of Christ. Each step you take is a stride of self-denial. The way is hard, just as Jesus foretold, but the promise drives you—this trail leads to life. If you walk in the light provided from the pinnacle of God's mountain, you will find yourself in fellowship with the One "who alone has immortality, who dwells in unapproachable light, whom no one has ever seen or can see" (1 Tim 6.16).

At the sheer magnificence of such a thought, you are compelled to ask with David, "Who shall ascend the hill of the Lord? And who shall stand in his holy place?" Forget Everest. Look higher than K2. Climbing those peaks doesn't even compare to this challenge.

The obvious question is, "Who is worthy of such a feat?" How can one be bound by the frailties of human existence and still reach that place where God invites him to enjoy the most precious form of community? If we pause and listen, perhaps we can hear the echoes that whisper with the winds from far above. "If anyone loves me, he will keep my word, and my Father will love him, and we will come to him and make our home with him" (John 14.23). But how?

David's answer is straightforward: "He who has clean hands

and a pure heart." Only the man who climbs with purity of action and singleness of motive can ascend Mount God. We might use the word **INTEGRITY** to summarize. The man of integrity will receive blessing from Jehovah and righteousness from the God of his salvation. Integrity characterizes the generation of those who seek him, who seek the face of the God of Jacob.

Isn't it interesting that Isaiah 2 and Psalm 24—both referencing the mountain of the Lord—refer to Jehovah as "the God of Jacob"? Of all the characters in all of God's Book, why Jacob? As we study the slopes of our own spiritual Currahee, let's pause for a moment, take a deep breath of the cool mountain air, and reflect on the significance of this reference. Why, on two different occasions in relation to ascending a mountain, "the God of Jacob"?

Jacob's Roots

Genesis 25.25–26 tells us of Jacob's birth to Isaac and Rebekah:

When her days to give birth were completed, behold, there were twins in her womb. The first came out red, all his body like a hairy cloak, so they called his name Esau. Afterward his brother came out with his hand holding Esau's heel, so his name was called Jacob.

At first glance, the name "Jacob" doesn't sound bad at all. It's a respectable and popular name in our own culture. However, as we dig a little deeper we discover that in Hebrew, "Jacob" means "he takes by the heel" or "he cheats." How would you like to have that name? "There goes 'He cheats.'" To bear that name for life would obviously be less than flattering. But truth be told, "Jacob" described this grandson of Abraham quite well. We'll notice just a few examples.

In Genesis 25.29–33 we are told how Jacob, the second-born son of Isaac, was able to lay claim to the treasured birthright—a special double-portion of his father's material possessions reserved exclusively for the firstborn son.

Once when Jacob was cooking stew, Esau came in from the field, and he was exhausted. And Esau said to Jacob, "Let me eat some of that red stew, for I am exhausted!" ...Jacob said, "Sell me your birthright now." Esau said, "I am about to die; of what use is a birthright to me?" Jacob said, "Swear to me now." So he swore to him and sold his birthright to Jacob.

As a result, Jacob conveniently manipulated his way into the privileged position of the firstborn. However, in order to actually receive the double blessing from his father, he had to cheat.

Genesis 27 reveals Jacob's plan—with the help of Rebekah, his mother—to deceive his father into believing that he was, in fact, Esau. Isaac's eyes had grown "dim so that he could not see" (Gen 27.1). As Jacob came to his father, Isaac asked, "Who are you?" and Jacob was willing to blatantly lie: "I am Esau your firstborn" (Gen 27.18–19). He even had the audacity to utter the name of Jehovah in supporting his lie—"the LORD your God granted me success" (Gen 27.20). Before the scene is left, Jacob had received the cherished gift. But at what cost?

By the time Esau realized what had happened, his father was helpless to change what had already been done: "'Your brother came deceitfully, and he has taken away your blessing.' Esau said, 'Is he not rightly named Jacob? For he has cheated me these two times. He took away my birthright, and behold, now he has taken away my blessing'" (Gen 27.35–36).

Genesis 27.41–43 details how this family was ripped apart at the seams by envy and deception.

> Now Esau hated Jacob because of the blessing with which his father had blessed him, and Esau said to himself, "The days of mourning for my father are approaching; then I will kill my brother Jacob." But the words of Esau her older son were told to Rebekah. So she sent and called Jacob her younger son and said to him, "Behold, your brother Esau comforts himself about you by planning to kill you. Now therefore, my son, obey my voice. Arise, flee to Laban my brother in Haran and stay with him a while, until your brother's fury turns away."

Jacob had been doubly blessed, but now he was forced to run for his life.

Before we take another step, it's important for you to notice something about Jacob and his relationship with the Creator. We've already noted, in Genesis 27.20, Jacob's choice of words as he talked with his father: "the LORD *your* God." It's evident that Isaac had claimed allegiance to Jehovah. Before Jacob departed, in Genesis 28.3, Isaac referred to Jehovah as *El Shaddai* in Hebrew, or "God Almighty." Jacob's father believed in God, but note the lack of any indication that Jacob himself had made faith in God his own.

Jacob Begins to Grow

At this point, let's just listen to the Biblical account from Genesis 28.10–22:

Jacob left Beersheba and went toward Haran. And he came to a certain place and stayed there that night, because the sun had set. Taking one of the stones of the place, he put it under his head and lay down in that place to sleep. And he dreamed, and behold, there was a ladder set up on the earth, and the top of it reached to heaven. And behold, the angels of God were ascending and descending on it! And behold, the LORD stood above it and said, "I am the LORD, the God of Abraham your father and the God of Isaac. The land on which you lie I will give to you and to your offspring. Your offspring shall be like the dust of the earth, and you shall spread abroad to the west and to the east and to the north and to the south, and in you and your offspring shall all the families of the earth be blessed. Behold, I am with you and will keep you wherever you go, and will bring you back to this land. For I will not leave you until I have done what I have promised you." Then Jacob awoke from his sleep and said, "Surely the LORD is in this place, and I did not know it." And he was afraid and said, "How awesome is this place! This is none other than the house of God, and this is the gate of heaven.

So early in the morning Jacob took the stone that he had put under his head and set it up for a pillar and poured oil on the top of it. He called the name of that place Bethel. …Then Jacob made a vow, saying, "If God will be with me and will keep me in this way that I go, and will give me bread to eat and clothing to

wear, so that I come again to my father's house in peace, then the
LORD shall be my God."

Again, notice carefully the terminology. Jehovah presented
himself as "the God of Abraham your father and the God of
Isaac." In awe, Jacob confessed, "Surely the LORD is in this place,
and I did not know it." But as we all know, there's a big difference
between recognizing the existence of God and claiming him as
the ruler of one's life.

Before leaving Bethel, Jacob made a vow: "If God will be with
me … then the LORD shall be my God." It's clear that Jacob and
Jehovah had yet to come to fully trusting terms. Jacob needed
to grow up. Like each of us, he needed to pass through spiritual
Boot Camp. He had, however, begun the journey.

Little did Jacob know that a good portion of his own spiritual
Boot Camp would last for twenty years with his uncle Laban in
Haran. One fact became clear over those two decades—Jehovah
was with Jacob. It was evident, even to his uncle. Whatever Jacob
did, God made it to prosper. Two wives, two concubines, eleven
sons and one daughter later, "the LORD said to Jacob, 'Return to
the land of your fathers and to your kindred, and I will be with
you'" (Gen 31.3).

Notice, however, even after twenty years, the phraseology Jacob used. In speaking to his wives—"the God of my father has
been with me" (Gen 31.5). Such seems to have been a theme in
Jacob's vocabulary. He had heard about this God from his youth.
It was apparent that a Being beyond himself had greatly prospered
each step of his pilgrimage, but something was still missing. Even
Laban recognized Jehovah in the same way: "The God of your father spoke to me last night" (Gen 31.29). In Genesis 31.42, Jacob
affirmed that "the God of my father, the God of Abraham and
the Fear of Isaac" had been on his side. In Genesis 31.53, Jacob
called on "the God of Abraham and the God of Nahor, the God
of their father" to judge between himself and Laban. "So Jacob
swore by the Fear of his father Isaac."

Can you see the point? In Jacob's mind Jehovah was undoubtedly a God—the God of Abraham, the God of Nahor, the God of his forefathers. He would swear in fear by this God, but only by the fear of his father. Jacob had yet to approach the slopes of Currahee for himself.

In Genesis 32.9–11, as he was confronted with finally seeing his brother Esau face to face after twenty long years, Jacob stopped to call upon Jehovah.

> "O God of my father Abraham and God of my father Isaac, O LORD who said to me, 'Return to your country and to your kindred, that I may do you good,' I am not worthy of the least of all the deeds of steadfast love and all the faithfulness that you have shown to your servant, for with only my staff I crossed this Jordan, and now I have become two camps. Please deliver me from the hand of my brother, from the hand of Esau, for I fear him, that he may come and attack me, the mothers with the children."

Do you see it? Jacob was beginning to grow. He was advancing in his spiritual development. He had reached that pivotal point in every man's journey on the road to integrity—the realization of utter unworthiness and the dire need for the intercession of someone greater than himself. It would take one more test, however, to finally refine Jacob to the point of making faith in Jehovah his own.

Jacob Becomes Israel

> The same night he arose and took his two wives, his two female servants, and his eleven children, and crossed the ford of the Jabbok. He took them and sent them across the stream, and everything else he had. And Jacob was left alone. (Gen 32.22–24)

Remember the meaning of Currahee? "Stands alone." Jacob finally found himself standing at the base of his own personal Currahee.

> And a man wrestled with him until the breaking of the day. When the man saw that he did not prevail against Jacob, he touched his hip socket, and Jacob's hip was put out of joint as he wrestled with him. Then he said, "Let me go, for the day has broken." But

Jacob said, "I will not let you go unless you bless me." And he said to him, "What is your name?" And he said, "Jacob." Then he said, "Your name shall no longer be called Jacob, but Israel [He strives with God], for you have striven with God and with men, and have prevailed." Then Jacob asked him, "Please tell me your name." But he said, "Why is it that you ask my name?" And there he blessed him. So Jacob called the name of the place Peniel [the face of God], saying, "For I have seen God face to face, and yet my life has been delivered." (Gen 32.24–30)

From that point on, it's not hard to guess how Jacob referred to Jehovah. In Genesis 33.5, as he bowed before his brother Esau, Jacob spoke of the children "whom God has graciously given your servant." Did you notice the subtle change in description? Not the God of Abraham, Isaac, or Nahor. "These are the children whom God has graciously given me."

After 20 long years, Jacob had finally come home. Most significant of all, however, Jacob had finally climbed the mountain of God for himself. He had fled in fear, calling on the name of his father's God. Eventually he returned in faith, humbly surrendering himself as Jehovah's servant.

And Jacob came safely to the city of Shechem … and he camped before the city. And from the sons of Hamor, Shechem's father, he bought for a hundred pieces of money the piece of land on which he had pitched his tent. There he erected an altar and called it El-Elohe-Israel [God, the God of Israel]. (Gen 33.18–20)

Do you see the point? Remember, "Israel" was his new God-given name. As best I can tell, we have no record of Jacob ever referring to Jehovah as his God prior to wrestling throughout the night at Bethel. But as he wrestled, he climbed. As he climbed, he struggled. As he struggled, he matured. And as he matured, he came face to face with his Maker who changed his name. And you don't ever read of Jacob swearing by the fear of his father again. From that point on, Jehovah was his God, the God worthy of Jacob's worship and adoration.

To use the language of our illustration, Jacob had ascended

the mountain of the Lord. It wasn't easy. He certainly didn't arrive there by mistake. It took work. It required wrestling. It demanded purging out all that would ensnare and weigh him down. It called for the laying aside of sin. It was essential that Jacob turn himself completely over by faith to *El Shaddai*, God Almighty. But when he did, he found himself at the summit where God could transform him from deceiver to soldier, cheater to warrior, coward to patriarch.

On the summit of Currahee, Jacob became a leader in the truest sense of the word.

> So Jacob said to his household and to all who were with him, "Put away the foreign gods that are among you and purify yourselves and change your garments. Then let us arise and go up to Bethel, so that I may make there an altar to the God who answers me in the day of my distress and has been with me wherever I have gone." (Gen 35.2–3)

In what way could a man, a husband, a father more effectively lead than that?

Continued reading reveals that the Genesis narrative slowly shifts focus away at this point from Jacob to his son Joseph as the next great leader of Abraham's descendants. But Jacob's words at the end of his earthly journey are recorded for all time. Remember where he began: a deceiver and a cheater. Reflect on where he had been in his painful, wayward trek to the mountain of God. Finally, rejoice with him as he stands on the summit and summarizes his journey:

> "The God before whom my fathers Abraham and Isaac walked, the God who has been my shepherd all my life long to this day, the angel who has redeemed me from all evil, bless the boys; and in them let my name be carried on, and the name of my fathers Abraham and Isaac; and let them grow into a multitude in the midst of the earth." (Gen 48.15–16)

May God bless all fathers that they would be able to make such statements at the end of their own lives.

"This is the Generation..."

As we come back to our own journey, having caught our breath and noted the trail winding ahead, remember. Remember that both David and Isaiah, in speaking of ascending a mountain, refer to God as "the God of Jacob." Why Jacob? Why not Noah? What about Abraham? Who could overlook Moses?

While there might be more than one way to answer that question, could at least part of the secret lie behind God's vivid chronicle of Jacob's journey? Here was a man who had to wrestle. Every step of the way was a fight. Even when not fully realizing it, Jacob was engaged in a life-long struggle to reach and ascend the mountain of God. The tale of his transformation is remarkable. And if God could take the unrefined soul of Jacob and purify it for such a magnificent purpose, what about the potential for other souls?

As we probe the depths of that question, recall the words of David in Psalm 24.3–6:

> Who shall ascend the hill of the LORD?
>> And who shall stand in his holy place?
> He who has clean hands and a pure heart,
>> Who does not lift up his soul to what is false
>> And does not swear deceitfully.
> He will receive blessing from the LORD
>> And righteousness from the God of his salvation.
> Such is the generation of those who seek him,
>> Who seek the face of the God of Jacob.

Note David's use of the word *generation*. Allow that to sink in. They are words that echo true for every generation. Previous generations of soldiers have done what they could to press the battle forward, but the point holds true: "The righteous shall live by his faith" (Hab 2.4).

Herein lies a vital principle of the Boot Camp experience. You and I will not ascend the mountain of God by the faith of those who lived thousands of years ago. We will not make our way to the summit based on the hard work of our grandparents' generation. You and I are not taking steps upward as we merely talk about the trials of our parents. They waged their own battles. They had their own mountains to climb; now we stand on the brink of ours. Regardless of our spiritual heritage, you and I are not physically born on the mountain of God. We do not mystically and effortlessly find ourselves at its summit simply because our pictures are in the directory of a particular congregation.

Many battles of the past are just that—in the past. A number of past conflicts do not currently stand in our way of ascending the mountain of God. We learn from them, but our questions must be, "What is our Currahee? Where is the battle being waged in the 21st century?"

You have not been called to climb anyone else's mountain. You have been summoned to summit your own. You are blessed to be a part of the current generation of those who seek him, who seek the face of the God of Jacob. Listen to the battle cry.

> Lift up your heads, O gates!
>> And be lifted up, O ancient doors,
>> That the King of glory may come in.
> Who is this King of glory?
>> The LORD, strong and mighty,
>> The LORD, mighty in battle!
> Lift up your heads, O gates!
>> And lift them up, O ancient doors,
>> That the King of glory may come in.
> Who is this King of glory?
>> The LORD of hosts,
>> He is the King of glory!

He still exists. He says that there is still work to do. There is still a mountain to climb. It will not be attempted by those who lived decades, centuries or millennia ago. They are resting high on the mountain. Their work is done. Currahee now rises before you and God's assurance remains: "Be strong and courageous. Do not be frightened, and do not be dismayed, for the LORD your God is with you wherever you go" (Josh 1.9).

The trail stretches before you. "Come, let us go up to the

mountain of the LORD, to the house of the God of Jacob, that he may teach us his ways and that we may walk in his paths" (Mic 4.2). Are you willing? Are you ready?

3

A Few Good Men

What Exactly is Integrity?

The essence of true holiness is conformity to the nature
and will of God. (Samuel Lucas)

I'm writing amidst the giggles of my three-year-old daughter,
Chloe. She laughs like her mother. Yesterday I watched from
behind my computer screen as she quietly picked at her finger-
nails for ten minutes, just like her mother. Recently caught up in
a moment of childlike exasperation, she threw up her hands and
asked in all seriousness, "Can you believe it?"—one of my wife's
frequently used pet phrases.

My daughter's world very much revolves around her mother,
and vice versa. They've been inscribed on each other's hearts. In a
quiet moment a few nights ago, Chloe professed with the sincerity that only a child can muster, "Mama, I want to be like you
when I grow up." Place a picture of my wife as a little girl beside
my daughter's picture and the differences can be seen only in the
age of the paper. I am blessed to wake up with beautiful mirror
images each morning.

There is a deep, rich, spiritual truth behind the idea of a child
bearing the image of a parent. My Creator tells me that I have
been created in his image and he uses beautiful, sometimes inti-
mate figures to establish that fact. At a particularly difficult moment in biblical history, as Israel had sunk so low as to suggest,

"The Lord has forsaken me, and the Lord has forgotten me," Jehovah asks, "Can a woman forget her nursing child and have no compassion on the son of her womb? Even these may forget, but I will not forget you. Behold, I have inscribed you on the palms of My hands" (Isa 49.15–16, NASB).

Can I ever truly comprehend the glory of my original magnificence? At times I bask in the warmth of that question. Too frequently, however, I cower in shame over my failures and foolish willingness to follow the distractions of the Enemy away from the divine intention.

Who would my daughter be without the tender daily influence of her mother? She might bear the physical attributes that come from genetics, but what about her personality? What about her tone, her expressions, her reactions and little quirks drawn from hours in her mother's presence? In a very real sense, she would not be her mother's daughter.

And who am I without a vital, daily connection to my Creator? Without his counsel, I'm nothing but a shell. Being created in his image has little to do with the appearance of my physical body. Without his guidance, what optimism can this corrupt world provide for the days ahead? Without his presence in my life, I'm nothing more than an orphan. I'm separated from the very root of my existence.

But how must it make my Father feel when I consistently act like his child? Take a moment to meditate on Jehovah's promise in Isaiah 49. Do you think of him in those terms? If not, you're missing a life-giving piece of the puzzle of your existence. God's greatest desire is fulfilled when our greatest desire is to pattern ourselves after him in the smallest details of life. His heart overflows when we inscribe his blueprint on our hearts. True holiness is realized when we conform the way we think, the way we talk, and the way we act to the will of the Creator. "Be imitators of God, as beloved children" (Eph 5.1). Rather than a pestering annoyance, imitating our Father as little children is actually a sign of spiritual maturity. "Truly, I say to you, unless you turn and become like children, you will never enter the kingdom of heaven" (Matt 18.3).

Significantly, our English word *character* has old linguistic roots seemingly drawn straight out of the context of Isaiah 49. In ancient times, *character* or *characterize* implicitly meant "to write, print, portray, engrave, or inscribe; a distinctive mark; an imprint on the soul." We've already noted God's assurance that he has "inscribed" us on the palms of his hands. The question is, when he looks at my hands and my heart, can he see himself? Does he see character? Does he find integrity?

Jesus: Man as God Envisioned

It is to integrity that the apostle Paul calls us in Philippians 2.5–7: "Have this attitude in yourselves which was also in Christ Jesus, who, although He existed *in the form* of God, did not regard equality with God a thing to be grasped, but emptied Himself, taking the form of a bond-servant, and being made in the likeness of men" (NASB).

In describing Jesus, Paul uses the Greek word *morphe*, affirming a foundational principle of the Son's identity developed throughout the New Testament. In 2 Corinthians 4.4, he speaks of "Christ, who is the image of God." In Colossians 1.15, he describes Jesus as "the image of the invisible God." "He is the radiance of the glory of God and the exact imprint of his nature" according to Hebrews 1.3.

Just as a child is often described as bearing the image of his father, the Jesus of the gospels is the unmistakable "image" of the invisible God. As John stated in the introduction of his gospel, "No one has ever seen God; the only God, who is at the Father's side, he has made him known" (John 1.18). As we look at this image, in one sense, we look at God.

Coming back to Philippians 2, Paul's climactic point is that even though Jesus existed in the form of God, he willingly took "the form of a servant, being born in the likeness of men. And being found in human form, he humbled himself by becoming obedient to the point of death, even death on a cross" (2.7–8). Jesus became God's man among men. He identified himself with men by becoming one. Near the end of his life, he clearly restated one of the fundamental aspects of his purpose: "If you had known me, you would have known my Father also. From now on you do know him and have seen him" (John 14.7). The point? Our clearest glimpse of man as God envisioned—man with godly character, or the godly imprint—is found in Jesus of Nazareth.

Jesus: The Path to the Ideal

How does all of this relate to you and me? "He who sanctifies and those who are sanctified all have one origin. That is why he is not ashamed to call them brothers" and, "because he himself has suffered when tempted, he is able to help those who are being tempted" (Heb 2.11, 18).

Pause for a moment and think about being ashamed. Even today, have you done something for which you are ashamed? In a moment of awkwardness did you bend the truth? In a moment of weakness did you fantasize about a woman at work? In a moment of tension did you lose your temper and, as a result, the control of your tongue?

If you're like most of us, you have plenty of which to be ashamed—a long, ugly laundry list compiled over years of selfishness and rebellion. Perhaps the most recent addition to your list came just hours ago.

But isn't that what makes the promise of Hebrews 2 so special? A clearly defined path lies before each of us. It's admittedly difficult. The trail head is filled with signs which warn of the demanding slopes and strenuous climbs ahead.

> "The gate is narrow and the way is hard that leads to life, and those who find it are few." (Matt 7.14)

> "If anyone would come after me, let him deny himself and take up his cross daily and follow me." (Luke 9.23)

> "If anyone comes to me and does not hate his own father and mother and wife and children and brothers and sisters, yes, and even his own life, he cannot be my disciple. Whoever does not bear his own cross and come after me cannot be my disciple." (Luke 14.26–27)

"So therefore, any one of you who does not renounce all that he has cannot be my disciple." (Luke 14.33)

If we're honest with ourselves, we read those clearly defined "trail requirements" and are ready to hang our heads and walk away in shame. How can we hope to measure up? Too many times we've walked right by that narrow gate for a pathway of our own choosing. Sometimes we just don't want to deny ourselves. At times it's much easier to go along with the desires of those around us. What enjoyment could there possibly be in taking up a cross? When it comes right down to it, we don't want to give up control of all that we are and all that we have!

Pitifully armed with that self-realization, we're ready to "go away sorrowfully" like the rich young ruler of Matthew 19. But just as we begin to step away in defeat, the words of Hebrews 2 echo from within: "He who sanctifies and those who are sanctified all have one origin. That is why he is not ashamed to call them brothers…because he himself has suffered when tempted, he is able to help those who are being tempted."

Our King invites us to reconsider: "You aren't being called to travel this pathway alone. I've been there. I know the difficulties firsthand. I traveled the pathway flawlessly. I took it further than anyone ever has. I know about your failures. I can clearly see your weaknesses. But if you are willing to follow me, I will be your guide. I will lead you in this quest of renovating yourself to be everything that our Father has envisioned. Follow me, and I will unashamedly call you 'brother.'"

If we are ever to truly be the men God envisioned, we must take seriously the demanding words and inspiring example of the One who bore the "exact imprint" of the Father's nature. "There is salvation in no one else" (Acts 4.12). We must count the cost and appreciate what it will take to succeed. The only perfect image-bearer to ever live has defined the path. He has marked the boundaries, and as our King, he's not afraid to stretch and challenge us. Here he comes. Let's stand at attention and listen up.

A Matter of the Heart

"A sower went out to sow his seed. And as he sowed, some fell along the path and was trampled underfoot, and the birds of the air devoured it. And some fell on the rock, and as it grew up, it withered away, because it had no moisture. And some fell among thorns, and the thorns grew up with it and choked it. And some fell into good soil and grew and yielded a hundredfold. He who has ears to hear, let him hear." (Luke 8.5–8)

Right along with those who originally heard this parable, we scratch our heads and wonder what exactly our King means. To clarify, he continues,

"Now the parable is this: The seed is the word of God. The ones along the path are those who have heard. Then the devil comes and takes away the word from their hearts, so that they may not believe and be saved. And the ones on the rock are those who, when they hear the word, receive it with joy. But these have no root; they believe for a while, and in time of testing fall away. And as for what fell among the thorns, they are those who hear, but as they go on their way they are choked by the cares and riches and pleasures of life, and their fruit does not mature. As for that in the good soil, they are those who, hearing the word, hold it fast in an honest and good heart, and bear fruit with patience." (Luke 8.11–15)

The point? The seed is God's word and it is powerful.

For as the rain and the snow come down from heaven
 and do not return there but water the earth,
making it bring forth and sprout,
 giving seed to the sower and bread to the eater,
so shall my word be that goes out from my mouth;
 it shall not return to me empty,
but it shall accomplish that which I purpose,
 and shall succeed in the thing for which I sent it.
 (Isa 55.10–11)

The Creator has done his part in providing the revelation of his will. But the realization of God's intentions for my life depends upon which kind of soil the seed finds. In what condition is my heart? Does the seed have room to germinate therein? The environment the seed enters will ultimately shape the outcome of my response to God's vision.

Webster defines *integrity* as "steadfast adherence to a strict moral or ethical code; the state of being unimpaired; soundness; the quality or condition of being whole or undivided; completeness." Take a moment to slowly read over that definition again.

Isn't integrity exactly what Jesus is describing as he portrays those who hear the word of God, hold it fast in an honest and good heart, and bear fruit with patience? Remember spiritual Currahee from the last chapter?

> Who shall ascend the hill of the LORD?
>> And who shall stand in his holy place?
> He who has clean hands and a pure heart. (Psa 24.3–4)

Our King calls from the summit of spiritual Currahee for steadfast adherence to his revealed will. He seeks spiritual focus. He demands wisdom and good judgment. Energetic courage to do the right thing is essential, especially when the wrong thing is so much more convenient. Total dedication is an absolute requirement. But how will I respond when total dedication comes at the cost of total self-denial?

The Lord summons soldiers of integrity, and integrity begins with the heart. Integrity is a choice made within. How will I react as I hear his demands? My Father desires to make an imprint on my heart, the very idea behind the word *character*. But how will I respond when godly character comes at the cost of personal freedoms?

Think of the ancient practice of sealing letters with hot wax and a family seal. To ensure authenticity and ownership, the sender would imprint his "character" onto the outside of the envelope. Such is precisely what God desires to do within my life and on my heart. When people look at me, my Father desires that they would see him. That's what it means to "have the attitude in [ourselves] which was also in Christ Jesus" (Phil 2.5, NASB). But how will I respond when the attitude of Christ comes at the cost of suffering? "He who has ears to hear, let him hear."

Long ago, Jeremiah prophesied of a wonderful day which would be characterized by a new covenant: "But this is the covenant that I will make with the house of Israel after those days, declares the LORD: I will put my law within them, and I will write it on their hearts. And I will be their God, and they shall be my people" (Jer 31.33).

Hundreds of years later, the apostle Paul used the same figure in writing to the Corinthians: "And you show that you are a letter from Christ delivered by us, written not with ink but with the Spirit of the living God, not on tablets of stone but on tablets of human hearts" (2 Cor 3.3).

That's character—the message of God's Spirit engraved on the tablet of my heart. Integrity is founded within the heart of man. Its seed begins to sprout when I receive and wholeheartedly act upon the life-changing words of God, but I must realize that there is nothing that frustrates my Enemy more.

An Ancient Example

Imagine having a book of the Bible named after you. It doesn't just bear your name, it's your story. It chronicles your life—specifically, the way you've conducted yourself in the midst of the most difficult of situations. How would it be introduced? Try this example on for size and see if you wouldn't mind having the same kind of introduction to your book. "There was a man in the land of Uz whose name was Job, and that man was blameless and upright, one who feared God and turned away from evil" (Job 1.1).

It can't get much better than that, can it? The ancient narrative tells us that Job was "blameless." Literally, he was "complete" or "sound"—the very definition of *integrity*. "Blameless" corresponds with the word Jesus used in Matthew 5.48 when he said, "You therefore must be perfect, as your heavenly Father is perfect." To be *blameless* or *perfect* in a biblical context is to be "morally complete."

Secondly, Job was "upright." The word could also be rendered "straight." We might say "unimpaired" or "undivided." As Jehovah looked at Job, he saw a man who traveled the straight line of the divine intention. His eyes were firmly fixed on the goal and he had no plans of deviating from his stated course.

In a word, Job was a man of integrity, and that frustrated Satan to no end. Even after Job lost 7,000 sheep, 3,000 camels, 500 yoke of oxen, 500 female donkeys, a great many servants, seven sons and three daughters in one day, Jehovah was still able to ask Satan, "Have you considered my servant Job, that there is none like him on the earth, a blameless and upright man, who fears God and turns away from evil? He still holds fast his integrity" (Job 2.3). What a powerful example of courage to do the right thing even in the most difficult of circumstances!

Some of the book's most inspiring words are spoken later, as Job sat among his so-called friends with a torn robe, a shaved head, and loathsome sores from the sole of his foot to the crown of his head. Fresh from scraping himself with a piece of broken pottery while sitting in ashes, he authoritatively said, "As long as my breath is in me, and the spirit of God is in my nostrils, my lips will not speak falsehood, and my tongue will not utter deceit…till I die I will not put away my integrity from me" (Job 27.3–5).

Now, bring it back to your own Boot Camp experience. How would the book be introduced if it bore your name? How would it progress if it were written about you? Is your faith a frustration to the Adversary? Is your integrity a challenge to the Enemy? Has the divine imprint been definitively made? Will the roots of character help you to remain steadfast and immovable when the battle rages without and within?

As Job sits in that great "cloud of witnesses" we envisioned in Chapter 1, he is a testament of what can be. The invitation to which he responded still stands. "I am God Almighty; walk before me, and be blameless" (Gen 17.1). How you will you respond?

An Ongoing Journey

Ultimately, we must realize that more than a destination, integrity is an ongoing journey. It is a daily, sometimes difficult walk. The wise recorder of the Proverbs particularly pictures integrity in this light:

> Whoever walks in integrity walks securely, but he who makes his ways crooked will be found out. (Prov 10.9)
>
> The integrity of the upright guides them, but the crookedness of the treacherous destroys them. (Prov 11.3)
>
> Whoever walks in integrity will be delivered, but he who is crooked in his ways will suddenly fall. (Prov 28.18)

At times, we will all fall. Every climber does. But remember, we have a Guide who knows where he's going and what he's doing. He's the same Guide who empowered Paul to humbly confess,

> Not that I have already obtained this or am already perfect, but I press on to make it my own, because Christ Jesus has made me his own. Brothers, I do not consider that I have made it my own. But one thing I do: forgetting what lies behind and straining forward to what lies ahead, I press on toward the goal for the prize of the upward call of God in Christ Jesus. Let those of us who are mature think this way. (Phil 3.12–15)

Integrity is a journey—a journey that begins with one step in the right direction. That genuine first step must be chosen and taken by each one of us as individuals. We use the word "imagine" within this series because each of us as men has walked away from God. "All have sinned; all fall short of God's glorious standard" (Rom 3.23, NLT). But remember, the Creator "has put eternity into man's heart" (Ecc 3.11). He has blessed us with moral compasses to tell us when we've wandered away from the pathway. He has impressed within us the capacity to yearn for greater conformity to his will. He has granted us grace to make our imaginations reality.

> How can I search for beauty and truth unless that beauty and truth are already known to me in the depth of my heart? It seems that all of us human beings have deep inner memories of the paradise we have lost. Maybe the word "innocence" is better than

the word "paradise." We were innocent before we started feeling guilty; we were in the light before we entered into the darkness; we were at home before we started to search for a home. Deep in the recesses of our minds and hearts there lies hidden the treasure we seek. We know its preciousness, and we know that it holds the gift we most desire: a life stronger than death. [1]

There it is. Our ultimate objective. To rediscover the divine inscription, to definitively press it onto our hearts, and to unashamedly bear the image of our Father to his glory. He promises that you can rely on his guidance, that you can trust him when the battle is raging: "For the LORD gives wisdom; from his mouth come knowledge and understanding; he stores up sound wisdom for the upright; he is a shield to those who walk in integrity, guarding the paths of justice and watching over the way of his saints" (Prov 2.6–8).

Listen. Trust. Do what is necessary to advance as a soldier in heaven's kingdom and you will have aligned yourself with the ultimate Victor. You can exclaim with David,

By this I know that you delight in me:
    my enemy will not shout in triumph over me.
But you have upheld me because of my integrity,
    and set me in your presence forever. (Psa 41.11–12)

I started this chapter with my daughter, and I'll end it with her as well. Every once in a while, Chloe likes to compare the size and shape of her hands with mine. Her eyes fill with wonder as she tries to grasp the difference that only years can create. When she looks at my hands, in one sense she sees herself. She is inscribed there.

My Father also has hands. When he looks at his, he sees men of integrity. Does he see me? Does he see you?

4

The Lord's Infirmary

A Time to Heal

Be not wise in your own eyes; fear the LORD, and turn away from evil. It will be healing to your flesh and refreshment to your bones. (Prov 3.7–8)

"INSPECCCCTION!" We can easily picture the stereotypical grizzled Drill Sergeant bellowing the call to attention at the top of his lungs to a group of fledgling recruits. He realizes that inventory must be taken before any serious progress can be made. Before a ragtag group of rookies can be shaped into a refined and disciplined unit, progress must be gauged. What are the evident strengths? Where are the weaknesses? What should come easily? What could prove to be a real struggle?

Likewise, before a wet-behind-the-ears novice becomes a veteran soldier, he's got to be honest with himself. He may have come into his training very "wise in his own eyes." All of us have seen it. Perhaps we've even been Exhibit-A of the problem. Cockiness. Arrogance. An attitude that says "I'm the one who's gonna show everyone else how it's done."

Solomon very aptly described the man who believes he's already got it all together and isn't even interested in taking the necessary steps of spiritual conditioning.

The wise of heart will receive commandments, but a babbling fool will come to ruin. (Prov 10.8)

A fool takes no pleasure in understanding, but only in expressing his opinion. (Prov 18.2)

A fool's lips walk into a fight, and his mouth invites a beating. A fool's mouth is his ruin, and his lips are a snare to his soul. (Prov 18.6–7)

Do you see a man who is wise in his own eyes? There is more hope for a fool than for him. (Prov 26.12)

Sometimes, the wisest thing we can do is shut our mouths and look in the mirror. Honestly. Objectively. What good does it do to look into our own eyes and see our true selves as no one else does, but then act like nothing is wrong—especially when we know just how much needs to be improved?

Be doers of the word, and not hearers only, deceiving yourselves. For if anyone is a hearer of the word and not a doer, he is like a man who looks intently at his natural face in a mirror. For he looks at himself and goes away and at once forgets what he was like. But the one who looks into the perfect law, the law of liberty, and perseveres, being no hearer who forgets but a doer who acts, he will be blessed in his doing. (Jas 1.22–25)

Therein lies one of the greatest dangers in the war for your soul. It's time to step up and pay attention. Are you ready? Are you listening?

You can only look at yourself in the mirror and walk away unwilling to address your dirty laundry for so long before it doesn't bother you like it once did. In writing to Timothy, Paul warns of "the insincerity of liars whose consciences are seared" (1 Tim 4.2). They've looked. They've seen the great needs and embarrassing shortcomings. They know where improvement is expected by the Creator, but they've gotten to the point where they just don't care anymore. And as a result, they're living as liars.

Make no mistake. The man of integrity is willing to look squarely at himself in the mirror and ask the tough questions. The man of character will not only look intently into that mirror, but will walk away determined not to forget. The man of virtue refuses to go on lying to himself and his God. The man of strength will acknowledge his flaws, accept the Spirit's discipline, and do whatever is necessary to prepare his heart for the deep and distinctive imprint of the Creator. This is the man who will be blessed in his doing.

The first real step towards becoming the man God envisioned is a willingness to be honest with yourself. Do you even need to be healed?

Jesus' Work of Healing

When Jesus first stepped into the public spotlight of his own hometown, he began by simply reading from the prophet Isaiah:

> "The Spirit of the Lord is upon me,
>> because he has anointed me
>> to proclaim good news to the poor.
> He has sent me to proclaim liberty to the captives
>> and recovering of sight to the blind,
>> to set at liberty those who are oppressed,
>> to proclaim the year of the Lord's favor." (Luke 4.18–19)

As he elaborated, it became clear that his message was revolutionary. It was "good news" in the greatest of senses. Whereas the Jews had held to a year of Jubilee for generations, Jesus was going about announcing an age of Jubilee. God's Messiah had burst upon the scene. The kingdom of heaven was at hand. A new age had dawned, and one of its fundamental features was—and continues to be—the opportunity for healing.

Matthew documents how Jesus, early in his ministry, "went throughout all Galilee, teaching in their synagogues and proclaiming the gospel of the kingdom and healing every disease and every affliction among the people" (Matt 4.23). At a later point in the same gospel,

> Jesus went throughout all the cities and villages, teaching in their synagogues and proclaiming the gospel of the kingdom and healing every disease and every affliction. When he saw the crowds, he had compassion for them, because they were harassed

and helpless, like sheep without a shepherd. Then he said to his disciples, "The harvest is plentiful, but the laborers are few; therefore, pray earnestly to the Lord of the harvest to send out laborers into his harvest." (Matt 9.35–38)

In our present context, we might rephrase that last statement: pray earnestly to the Commander-in-Chief to send out soldiers onto the battlefield. Godly warriors are desperately needed in the fight against immorality, unbelief, false doctrine and all else that jeopardizes the souls of mankind.

But before the newest recruits hit the trenches, care must be taken to make sure they are fit for battle. They must be healthy and whole. Later on we'll spend some time in the Lord's armory, but before we get there, many of us have unresolved wounds below the surface. For the walking wounded, this first demands some time in the Lord's infirmary.

Self: A Deadly Traitor

As you reluctantly lay down on your own infirmary bed, imagine a great field of battle. At the moment, you're hunkered down with fellow kingdom soldiers. The sun has set, but the battle rages on. Explosions rattle your helmet and brighten the sky as if it were noon. The streaks of enemy bullets whizz by your head. Orders are being screamed up and down the line. You realize that this is what you have been trained to do. This is what Boot Camp was all about. This is where the battle is the hottest, where men show their mettle. The war for your soul and the souls of those you love is raging.

Finally, after what seems to have been an eternity's worth of waiting, the time comes to crawl out of the trench and confront the enemy head-on. Your objective is clear: gain the high ground, whatever the cost. A trumpet sounds. The Word of God leads the charge beneath the banners of heaven, his blood-soaked robe trailing in the wind. Warriors of the kingdom of light—flanking you to the right and left as far as the eye can see—rise as one. You courageously climb to your feet with a shout. And as you take your first steps forward, you're shot in the back—right through your heart.

But that doesn't make sense! The enemy is in front of you! In panic and confusion, you muster everything you have to turn around and see the traitorous culprit. Just before your eyes close and you take your last breath, you get a glimpse of the heartbreaking truth: a mirror image of yourself. *You* have shot your own self in the back.

Just a nightmare? A meaningless daydream? Not according to Paul, a veteran of the battlefield:

> So I find it to be a law that when I want to do right, evil lies close at hand. For I delight in the law of God, in my inner being, but I see in my members another law waging war against the law of my mind and making me captive to the law of sin that dwells in my members. Wretched man that I am! Who will deliver me from this body of death? (Rom 7.21–24)

There are times when the war is most intense within—a struggle to the death between my mind and my fleshly body. I know what is right. I know what the Commander demands. But I also know what I want, what I need, what makes me feel good. At times, the battle is so intense that I'm made to agonizingly scream with Paul, "Wretched man that I am!" Why do I continue to make the same mistakes? Why do I so easily compromise what I know to be right? Why do I betray myself and my God? Will I ever learn to stop shooting myself in the back? "Who will deliver me from this body of death?"

One thing is crystal clear. These self-inflicted wounds are real. They require more than the little bandage you've got in your gear. Even the field medic is at a loss. Your injuries are beyond a mere mortal's ability to mend. You're in desperate, life-threatening need and you feel yourself fading fast.

Then he appears. The Faithful with eyes like a flame of fire. The True whose voice is like the roar of many waters. While the conflict continues to rage all around, he calmly kneels at your side and confidently whispers that he has what you need. He can heal you. But you've got to decide whether or not to accept his offer. In order to be healed, you've got to go through some more pain. His blazing eyes look right into yours and he asks, "Do you trust me?" As you weakly nod your head, the sharp two-edged sword comes out of his mouth and he begins to go to work…

…On Your Hardened Heart

Jesus pointedly asked his disciples in Mark 8.17, "Do you not yet perceive or understand? Are your hearts hardened?" What is more serious than a heart too hardened to pump its own blood? Increasingly, warnings abound about what we eat, what we drink and how to be active enough to avoid the hardening of our arteries and killer heart disease later in life.

Much more serious, however, is the spiritual situation described in Hebrews 3.12–13: "Take care, brothers, lest there be in any of you an evil, unbelieving heart, leading you to fall away from the living God. But exhort one another every day, as long as it is called 'today,' that none of you may be hardened by the deceitfulness of sin."

Remember the message of Chapter 3? The problem with a spiritually insensitive heart is that it cannot be imprinted with the image God desires. It's like trying to make an impression in wax that has already dried or trying to trace your initials in concrete that has already hardened.

If we are ever to be useful to the Lord, our hearts must be heated once again. Our minds must be refined in the fire. We must allow the sharp sword of the Spirit to cut strong and cut deep.

> Now this I say and testify in the Lord, that you must no longer walk as the Gentiles do, in the futility of their minds. They are darkened in their understanding, alienated from the life of God because of the ignorance that is in them, due to their hardness of heart. They have become callous and have given themselves up to sensuality, greedy to practice every kind of impurity. But that is not the way you learned Christ!—assuming that you have heard about him and were taught in him, as the truth is in Jesus, to put off your old self, which belongs to your former manner of life and is corrupt through deceitful desires, and to be renewed in the spirit of your minds, and to put on the new

self, *created after the likeness of God* in true righteousness and holiness. (Eph 4.17–24)

There's the goal, clearly defined—to be recreated in newness of life after the likeness of God in authentic righteousness and holiness. "Imagine a man of integrity," Paul encourages. But the cost is also authoritatively stated. My hardened heart, my darkened understanding, my selfish life of impurity must be completely surrendered to the Master.

The Temptation to Mix Standards

As a man of integrity, I must make the choice to stop mixing standards. Too many of us continue in our sins because we've never fully made the decision to change. We want the end reward of the soldier of the cross as long as the personal cost isn't too great.

Consider these very personal words from Fred Stoeker in *Every Man's Battle* as sexual temptation is specifically addressed:

> God desired more for me. He had freed me from the pit, but I'd stopped moving toward Him. Having seen the prices I paid and my distance from God, I decided it was time to move closer.
>
> I expected the journey to be easy. After all, I had decided to eliminate pornography and affairs, and they were gone. I figured I could stop the rest of this sexual junk just as easily.
>
> But I couldn't. Every week I said I wouldn't look at those [lingerie] ad inserts, but every Sunday morning the striking photos compelled me. Every week I'd vow to avoid watching R-rated "sexy" movies when I traveled, but every week I'd fail, sweating out tough battles and always losing. Every time I gazed at some glistening jogger, I'd promise to never do it again. But I always did.
>
> What I'd done was simply trade the pornography of *Playboy* and *Gallery* for the pornography of ad inserts and other magazine ads. The affairs? I'd simply traded the physical liaisons for mental affairs and daydreams—affairs of the eyes and heart. The sin remained because I'd never really changed, never rejected sexual sin, never escaped sexual slavery. I'd merely exchanged masters.
>
> A couple of months slipped by, then a couple of years. The distance from God grew wider, the bills stacked higher, and my

impurity still ruled me. My faith waned further with each failure. Each desperate loss caused more desperation. While I could
always say no, I could never mean no.

Something was gripping me, something relentless, something mean.[1]

The problem? A divided heart. With each day of compromise
it grows harder. The sense of defeat? It stems from a darkened
mind that with each venture into sensuality grows darker. The
feelings of alienation from the Creator? A natural result of deceitful desires that continue to be selfishly gratified while the God-
given conscience is drowned out.

Now, contrast those feelings of absolute despair with the example of 26-year-old King Josiah following the discovery of the
ancient Book of the Law.

> Then the king sent and gathered together all the elders of Ju-
> dah and Jerusalem. And the king went up to the house of the
> LORD, with all the men of Judah and the inhabitants of Jerusa-
> lem and the priests and the Levites, all the people both great and
> small. And he read in their hearing all the words of the Book
> of the Covenant that had been found in the house of the LORD.
> And the king stood in his place and made a covenant before the
> LORD, to walk after the LORD and to keep his commandments
> and his testimonies and his statutes, with all his heart and all
> his soul, to perform the words of the covenant that were written
> in the book. …And Josiah took away all the abominations from
> all the territory that belonged to the people of Israel and made
> all who were present in Israel serve the LORD their God. All his
> days they did not turn away from following the LORD, the God
> of their fathers. (2 Chron 34.29–33)

Did you pick up on the key word of the passage? Josiah was
willing to go *"all"* the way in his battle for integrity. He had
counted the cost and was willing to pay it. He had heard the
Master's demands and courageously volunteered for service. With
his whole heart he was dedicated to the will of the Almighty, and
it came through loud and clear in his actions.

Isn't the difference dramatic? Aren't our own options also evident? Make those options personal to your own walk of discipleship. Will you simply exchange one form of impurity for another or will you "stand" in your "place" and make a covenant before the Lord? Will you maintain a "divided" heart or will you promise to "walk after the Lord" with all of your heart and all of your soul? Will you continue to tolerate the idols of immaturity and sensuality that have taken hold of your affections or will you thoroughly cleanse all of the "abominations" from "all of the territory" of your life?

Here's the point. Men of mixed standards are not yet men of integrity. The divine imprint of godly character has yet to be definitively made. Men of integrity hear the call for a decision and are ready and willing to make it.

"Now therefore fear the LORD and serve him in sincerity and in faithfulness" (Josh 24.14). Our English word *sincerity* is from the same root word as *integrity*. It inherently means "complete, sound, blameless." Men of integrity completely and wholly serve the Lord in sincerity. They listen to the call to "put away the gods that your fathers served ... and serve the LORD. And if it is evil in your eyes to serve the LORD, choose this day whom you will serve" (Josh 24.14–15). Men of integrity rise as one to their feet having made that decision.

Men of integrity listen to Joshua and realize that men of mixed standards "are not able to serve the LORD, for he is a holy God. He is a jealous God; he will not forgive your transgressions or your sins. If you forsake the LORD and serve foreign gods, then he will turn and do you harm and consume you, after having done you good" (Josh 24.19–20). Men of integrity look into the mirror of God's word and act from a willingness to "put away the foreign gods" that are among them and to "incline" their "hearts to the LORD, the God of Israel" (Josh 24.23).

The question is, are you a man of integrity? If not, are you willing to set aside the excuses and the double-mindedness? How long do you intend to remain ensnared? How long must your family and friends wait before they can depend upon your wholehearted determination to serve the Lord? How long before you can look your God in the eye?

Too many times we have shot ourselves in the back. Realize that Jesus, the Master Healer, has found us on the battlefield and offers us the opportunity to "abide in him, so that when he appears we may have confidence and not shrink from him in shame at his coming. If you know that he is righteous, you may be sure that everyone who practices righteousness has been born of him" (1 John 2.28–29).

For too long we have lived like "double-minded men, unstable" in all our ways (Jas 1.8). Our King, armed with the ability to heal, looks at our self-inflicted wounds and shows us a better way.

> By this we shall know that we are of the truth and reassure our heart before him; for whenever our heart condemns us, God is greater than our heart, and he knows everything. Beloved, if our heart does not condemn us, we have confidence before God; and whatever we ask we receive from him, because we keep his commandments and do what pleases him. ...Whoever keeps his commandments abides in him, and he in them. And by this we know that he abides in us, by the Spirit whom he has given us. (1 John 3.19–24)

What is required to "abide in" the ultimate Victor? The crucifixion of my old self.

> Put to death therefore what is earthly in you: sexual immorality, impurity, passion, evil desire, and covetousness, which is idolatry. On account of these the wrath of God is coming. In these you too once walked, when you were living in them. But now you must put them all away: anger, wrath, malice, slander, and obscene talk from your mouth. Do not lie to one another, seeing that you have put off the old self with its practices and have put on the new self, which is being renewed in knowledge *after the image of its creator.* (Col 3.5–10)

Could the point be any clearer? Imagine man as God envisioned—a man renewed after the image of his Creator! But do more than just imagine. Resolve to be that man by reclaiming the sinfully divided territory of your heart and putting your old rebellious self to death.

"Today This Scripture Has Been Fulfilled in Your Hearing"

Think back to the synagogue scene of Luke 4 we referenced at the beginning of this chapter.

> "The Spirit of the Lord is upon me,
>   because he has anointed me
>   to proclaim good news to the poor.
> He has sent me to proclaim liberty to the captives
>   and recovering of sight to the blind,
>   to set at liberty those who are oppressed,
>   to proclaim the year of the Lord's favor." (Luke 4.18–19)

In this age of Jubilee, Jesus has a proclamation of good news for *the poor*. Recognize that the poor of this age can include people of all social grades whose lives are impoverished by their failure to know and love the Source of their blessings.

The Christ speaks to those whose lives are deprived by their proud self-sufficiency. He invites those who are socially rich, but poor in good works. He beckons those who are materially wealthy, but lacking in compassion. "Blessed are the poor in spirit," he says, "for theirs is the kingdom of heaven" (Matt 5.3). He stands over self-wounded human beings and mercifully offers a better way. "You must reach the end of your rope. To follow me, you must hit the bottom of your spiritual pockets and turn them inside out. But you can be blessed. When you realize that you will never be truly happy until you confess your spiritual bankruptcy, when you wholeheartedly seek what only I can provide in your life, you will find the answer." You are blessed when you cry out with David, "The Lord is near to the brokenhearted and saves the crushed in spirit" (Psa 34.18).

In this age, the *captives* may walk about quite freely, but be in severe bondage to selfishness, anger, bitterness, lust, greed and fear of the future. Our King waves the banner of Jubilee and proclaims throughout the battlefield, "Truly, truly, I say to you, everyone who commits sin is a slave to sin. The slave does not remain in the house forever; the son remains forever. So if the Son sets you free, you will be free indeed" (John 8.34–36). How foolish to even think of walking onto a field of battle with shackles around our hands and feet!

In this age, the *blind* may have perfect 20/20 vision, and yet not see the greatest weaknesses and deficiencies of their own lives. Jesus invites those who are living by sight, not by faith. He offers to restore real vision as he counsels us all to buy from him "salve to anoint your eyes, so that you may see" (Rev 3.18). How ridiculous to think that we could wage a war without clear vision!

In this age, the *oppressed* may appear to be in control—to lead attractive, carefree lives. Inwardly, all the while, they are unhappy, discontent, unsatisfied and miserable. Why? Because they are still slaves to the great Adversary of the soul. But Jesus has come! The gracious cry of Jubilee is made throughout the battlefield for all to hear: "The Lord is a stronghold for the oppressed, a stronghold in times of trouble" (Psa 9.9).

Here is the key: Jesus is seeking more than mere students. The time comes when each of us is called to step out of the classroom and onto the battlefield. We make a mistake when quoting Luke 9.23 if we divorce it from the context of the previous verse. Such is not a "Scriptural divorce." Jesus had just stated, "The Son of Man must suffer many things and be rejected by the elders and chief priests and scribes, and be killed, and on the third day be raised."

It is in the very next verse that he says to all, "If anyone would come after me, let him deny himself and take up his cross daily and follow me."

Jesus of Nazareth always comes asking disciples to follow him. There is a difference in "accepting" him and following him. To "believe" in him is a start, but Jesus is looking for followers. To "worship" him is commendable, but following him can cost so much more. How many millions "worship" Jesus without ever following him?

Simply stated, I will either follow the glorified Christ onto the battlefield of the soul or I won't. If I follow him, I will follow him in the context of death. Borrowing Jesus' language and placing it in modern phraseology, I will either deny self and subject it to the death penalty daily, or I will not. Sexual immorality and impurity? They must be strapped into the electric chair. Envy, strife and jealousy? It's time for a lethal injection. Fits of anger, selfishness and rivalries? Hang 'em and hang 'em high.

Our King is looking for more than just admiring students; students don't turn the tide of a war. He is seeking followers. He is recruiting warriors. This is an all-or-nothing proposition every single day. It involves your whole heart. Your entire being. As such, it impacts every aspect of your life. There is no task, no arena, no realm, no conversation, no project, no deal, no relationship, no politic nor philosophy in which you can exclude his Lordship. He is either Lord of all—including your life—or he is someone who is just passing by on the battlefield. And as he passes by, if you refuse his healing intercession on your behalf, you are doomed to a lonely death and a hopeless eternity—lost on the battleground of your soul.

One day, regardless of your decision, you will come face to face with him and you will be held accountable. "If one wished to contend with him, one could not answer him once in a thousand times. He is wise in heart and mighty in strength—who has hardened himself against him, and succeeded?" (Job 9.4).

In the meantime, you have a choice.

Savor the irony. In order to heal ourselves, we've got to crucify all elements of our rebellious existence, beginning with our egoistic, back-stabbing, traitorous selves. Only then will we be truly fit for battle and completely useful to the King. Only then will we reach the potential our God has always intended. Only then will we be able to say with Paul,

> I have been crucified with Christ. It is no longer I who live, but Christ who lives in me. And the life I now live in the flesh I live by faith in the Son of God, who loved me and gave himself for me. (Gal 2.20)

O to be like Thee! Blessed Redeemer:
This is my constant longing and prayer;
Gladly I'll forfeit all of earth's treasures,
Jesus, Thy perfect likeness to wear.

O to be like Thee! Full of compassion,
Loving, forgiving, tender and kind,
Helping the helpless, cheering the fainting,
Seeking the wandering sinner to find.

O to be like Thee! Lowly in spirit,
Holy and harmless, patient and brave;
Meekly enduring cruel reproaches,
Willing to suffer, others to save.

O to be like Thee! Lord, I am coming,
Now to receive th'anointing divine;
All that I am and have I am bringing;
Lord, from this moment all shall be Thine.

O to be like Thee! O to be like Thee!
Blessed Redeemer, pure as Thou art;
Come in Thy sweetness, come in Thy fullness;
Stamp Thine own image deep on my heart.

"O To Be Like Thee," Thomas O. Chisholm

Part Two

As Integrity is Born, What Must be Put to Death?

God's truth stands firm like a foundation stone with this inscription:

"The Lord knows those who are his,"

and

"Those who claim they belong to the Lord must turn away from all wickedness."

2 Timothy 2.19, NLT

5

Selfishness

The Struggle Against Our Own Affections

He died for all, that those who live might no longer live for themselves but for him who for their sake died and was raised. (2 Cor 5.15)

Two soldiers with hands shaking and hearts racing can finally catch their breath. They've been in this trench for days. They've fought for what seems like years. They've seen things their young minds could not possibly have imagined just months ago.

One is from Kansas. He grew up on a dairy farm. Prior to being shipped out, the scariest thing he had ever done was propose to his highschool sweetheart. She said "yes" the day before he left the country. Now, as he does his best to stay alive, she shops for a wedding dress, armed with an engagement ring and his promise to come home.

The other soldier hails from midtown New York. He's made mistakes. He's wasted plenty. He's ready to go back home, but he burned all his bridges before he left. No one writes to him here. His only family are his fellow soldiers and most of them keep their distance. He's bitter—seems like he always has been. He's lonely, but he won't admit it. He's not sure how he got here, he just remembers that joining the military seemed like the right thing to do at the time.

Kansas and New York have fought side by side in the same

trench for twelve long hours. Mercifully, the sounds of war seem to have steadied. An uneasy calm whispers with the wind. Both find it hard to relax. Both know they should try. Neither can tell how long it will be before the quiet erupts into chaos once more. Both acknowledge that it won't be long enough.

Kansas' hand naturally reaches into his pocket and pulls out a pitifully crumpled picture of his small-town sweetheart. He wonders what she's doing at this moment. He daydreams of a future on a few acres back in Kansas. Three kids. A dog. The two of them, just sitting on a front porch swing for hours.

New York asks him what he's looking at. Kansas slowly turns the faded photo around with a sheepish grin. He blushes. He can't help but talk about how lucky he is. As Kansas speaks of wedding plans, New York's mind wanders home as well. What will it be like to step off the ship that brings him back home with no one there to greet him?

In that instant, something glances off of New York's left shoulder and slowly rolls to a stop two feet behind him. As his mind struggles to process what just happened, he sees Kansas lunging forward. He has trouble understanding as Kansas elbows him in the ribs and shoves him aside. In a flash, his ears ring with the sound of a horrible half-thud, half-explosion. As his head swivels, his eyes come to rest on what remains of Kansas who landed squarely—just as intended—on an enemy grenade.

"While We Were Still Weak…"

You've heard the stories. You remember the scenes in movies. Perhaps you're alive today because someone stepped up—when no one else could—for your father or grandfather in a similar situation. But above all, as Christians, we can each relate more than we initially realize.

> For while we were still weak, at the right time Christ died for the ungodly. For one will scarcely die for a righteous person—though perhaps for a good person one would dare even to die—but God shows his love for us in that while we were still sinners, Christ died for us. (Rom 5.6–8)

Stirring accounts abound of soldiers willing to make the ultimate sacrifice for their brothers in arms. Tales of fathers willing to forfeit everything for the welfare of their families carry the power to touch even the toughest of men. But what sense does it make for a warrior to give his life for his enemies?

Enter Jesus. He watched from heaven as Satan's grenade landed among the Creator's image-bearers. He consented to being born so that he might die. He endured temptation so that we could experience victory. He knew betrayal so that we might know divine faithfulness. His hands were bound so that we could go free. He stood alone so that we might have an Intercessor. He was wounded so that we could be healed. He was nailed to a cross so that we might escape condemnation.

"At the right time Christ died for the ungodly." We were all, each of us, prisoners of war on the wrong side of the battlefield with the righteous wrath of God looming large against us. And rightfully so. By our willingness to listen to Satan rather than our Creator, we had aligned ourselves with the Adversary. We were prisoners, yes, but prisoners of our own rebellious making. The bait was offered and we willingly took it. Sin closed the shackles around us, iniquity bound us behind enemy territory, and all hope was lost.

Then Jesus crossed the battlefield. At just the right time, he lowered himself into the Enemy's battle trench. He could have summoned more than twelve legions of angels to do his bidding, but he jumped on that unholy grenade himself to demonstrate once and for all the unrivaled love of God for mankind. Self-preservation may be the first law of nature, but self-sacrifice is the highest rule of grace.

It's no wonder, then, that the divine revelation calls for a response from the rescued. "For the love of Christ controls us, because we have concluded this: that one has died for all, therefore all have died; and he died for all, that those who live might no longer live for themselves but for him who for their sake died and was raised" (2 Cor 5.14–15).

We are called to be citizens of the kingdom of light, transformed by the grace of God, surrendering ourselves to the control of Christ. Our very character is to be reshaped after the image of the Creator. But in order for such to be even a possibility, certain all-too-natural characteristics must be put to death.

Where does the revolution begin? With selfishness. God's holy war of redemption commences with the battle over self. Here is the gap in the line, the flank, the epicenter of the Enemy's attack. Fail on this front, and all else will be lost.

At the heart of the gospel is the truth that Jesus has given himself so that I might die to myself. He has crossed the battlefield. He has invaded the Enemy's territory. By his sacrifice, he has cleared a pathway back to the ranks of the redeemed. Above the clamor of spiritual warfare and worldly distraction, he calls for godly soldiers who are willing to leave self-centeredness behind in the trenches of Satan. "If anyone would come after me, let him deny himself and take up his cross and follow me. For whoever would save his life will lose it, but whoever loses his life for my sake will find it" (Matt 16.24–25).

Casualties on the Ancient Battlefield

Konrad Heiden rightly said, "Those who wish to transform the world must first be able to transform themselves."[1] With that in mind, imagine a spectrum of attitude and action labeled SELF. On one extreme is complete self-denial. It is here that godly reason absolutely reigns over human passions and desires. Self-will has given way to self-control. Selfishness has been laid on the altar as a sacrifice to the Father. Self-centeredness has been replaced by God-centeredness. A man functioning on this end of the spectrum is truly able to say with Paul, "I have been crucified with Christ. It is no longer I who live, but Christ who lives in me" (Gal 2.20).

On the other extreme of the spectrum is completely unbridled lust. On this end, passion rules over reason. Human desires trump divine revelation. Self is gratified and the Christ is denied. Ego is exalted and the Creator is scorned.

Between the two extremes? The ancient battlefield of every human being.

Adam and Eve were the first to fight and die on this battlefield. Almighty God said, "You may surely eat of every tree of the garden, but of the tree of the knowledge of good and evil you shall not eat, for in the day that you eat of it you shall surely die" (Gen 2.16–17). The serpent said, "You will not surely die" (Gen 3.4). Behold the battlefield:

> When the woman saw that the tree was good for food, and that it was a delight to the eyes, and that the tree was to be desired to make one wise, she took of its fruit and ate, and she also gave some to her husband who was with her, and he ate. (Gen 3.6)

Human desires trumped divine revelation and the rippling aftershocks were catastrophic. "Sin came into the world through one man, and death through sin, and so death spread to all men because all sinned" (Rom 5.12).

Cain and Abel followed Adam and Eve onto the battlefield. Both offered sacrifices to God. The Creator was pleased with Abel's offering, but not with Cain's. Cain responded by murdering his brother Abel. Passion ruled over reason.

Genesis documents the rise and fall of one generation after another. As time passed, the crowning glory of God's creation—his image-bearers—only degenerated in their depravity. Eventually, "The LORD saw that the wickedness of man was great in the earth, and that every intention of the thoughts of his heart was only evil continually" (Gen 6.5). Self continued to be shamelessly gratified and the Creator was made to grieve.

Walk this battlefield in your mind. The Scriptures are our guide through mankind's sad self-centered history. The tower of Babel. Sodom. Joseph's brothers. Pharaoh. The rebellious children of Israel. Nadab. Abihu. Achan. Saul. Rehoboam. Jeroboam. Ahab. Gehazi. Nebuchadnezzar. Herod. Judas. Pilate. Ananias. Simon the magician. Felix the governor. Agrippa the king. Demas. Alexander the coppersmith. Diotrephes. Each of them serve as ancient examples recorded "for our instruction" (Rom 15.4). Why? Because we've been promised that things on this side of eternity aren't going to get any better.

Understand this, that in the last days there will come times of difficulty. For people will be lovers of self, lovers of money, proud, arrogant, abusive, disobedient to their parents, ungrateful, unholy, heartless, unappeasable, slanderous, without self-control, brutal, not loving good, treacherous, reckless, swollen with conceit, lovers of pleasure rather than lovers of God, having the appearance of godliness, but denying its power. (2 Tim 3.1–5)

The battle that began with Adam and Eve continues to rage on. The fronts of the war abound—sexual immorality, idolatry, jealousy, anger, sins of the tongue, hypocrisy, pride—but all are founded upon the corrupt bedrock of selfishness.

We should not be surprised, then, by the straightforward message of coming judgment which specifically identifies the consequences of exalting self above the Creator.

He will render to each one according to his works: to those who by patience in well-doing seek for glory and honor and immortality, he will give eternal life; but for those who are self-seeking and do not obey the truth, but obey unrighteousness, there will be wrath and fury. There will be tribulation and distress for every human being who does evil, the Jew first and also the Greek, but glory and honor and peace for everyone who does good, the Jew first and also the Greek. For God shows no partiality. (Rom 2.6–11)

The commission for the soldier of the cross? "He died for all, that those who live might no longer live for themselves but for him who for their sake died and was raised" (2 Cor 5.15). It's time to stop living for myself. It's not about me. The world doesn't revolve around me. "For thus says the LORD, who created the heavens (he is God!), who formed the earth and made it (he established it; he did not create it empty, he formed it to be inhabited!): 'I am the LORD, and there is no other'" (Isa 45.18).

The battle for my soul will turn on whether or not I consistently march in cadence with that message.

War against Our Affections

In Chapter 3 we emphasized that more than a destination,

integrity is an ongoing journey—a daily, sometimes difficult walk. No one understood that fact more clearly than the apostle Peter who emphasized the same point in his second letter to disciples of Christ.

> His divine power has granted to us all things that pertain to life and godliness, through the knowledge of him who called us to his own glory and excellence, by which he has granted to us his precious and very great promises, so that through them you may become partakers of the divine nature, having escaped from the corruption that is in the world because of sinful desire. (2 Pet 1.3–4)

As Christians, we've been called to share in the glory and excellence of Almighty God. Don't just read over that thought. Make it personal. You have been called to spiritual excellence! You have been summoned for fellowship with the Source of all glory. But you can't enjoy these blessings with one foot in the unshakeable kingdom of God and one foot resting on the shifting sands of self-interest. Our Father has made precious and very great promises to his children. He has provided the means whereby we might become partakers of the divine nature. This pathway of integrity lies ever present as one fork in our daily journey through this world. Each day we face the choice of self-indulgence or self-denial.

> So then, brothers, we are debtors, not to the flesh, to live according to the flesh. For if you live according to the flesh you will die, but if by the Spirit you put to death the deeds of the body, you will live. For all who are led by the Spirit of God are sons of God. For you did not receive the spirit of slavery to fall back into fear, but you have received the Spirit of adoption as sons, by whom we cry, "Abba! Father!" The Spirit himself bears witness with our spirit that we are children of God, and if children, then heirs—heirs of God and fellow heirs with Christ, provided we suffer with him in order that we may also be glorified with him. (Rom 8.12–17)

Just as Jesus is "the exact imprint" of the nature of God, we are invited to partake in the divine nature by stamping His holy image on our hearts. Just as our divine elder brother sacrificed self to the glory of God, so we also—as adopted sons of the righteous Father—are debtors to live according to the marching orders of the Spirit. Just as he is an heir, we can confidently exult in God's grace as fellow heirs, provided we suffer with him.

> Let fame, that all hunt after in their lives,
> Live register'd upon our brazen tombs
> And then grace us in the disgrace of death;
> When, spite of cormorant devouring Time,
> The endeavor of this present breath may buy
> That honor which shall bate his scythe's keen edge
> And make us heirs of all eternity.
> Therefore, brave conquerors—for so you are,
> That war against your own affections
> And the huge army of the world's desires—
> If you are arm'd to do as sworn to do,
> Subscribe to your deep oaths, and keep it too. [2]

"Brothers, be all the more diligent to make your calling and election sure" (2 Pet 1.10). As a Christian, you've sworn a deep oath of faithfulness to your Father. The Spirit himself bears witness with your spirit that you are his child, his heir. But in order to become a forgiven heir of the King, you were washed in the blood of God's Lamb. Now that blood quite naturally attracts the attention of the Adversary who "prowls around like a roaring lion, seeking someone to devour" (1 Pet 5.8). With the Spirit as your Guide and Christ as your Lord, you won't have to "fall back into fear," but you must quit trying to blaze your own trail.

> What causes quarrels and what causes fights among you? Is it not this, that your passions are at war within you? You desire and do not have, so you murder. You covet and cannot obtain, so you fight and quarrel. You do not have, because you do not ask. You ask and do not receive, because you ask wrongly, to spend it on your passions. You adulterous people! Do you not know that friendship with the world is enmity with God? Therefore whoever wishes to be a friend of the world makes himself an enemy of God. (Jas 4.1–4)

What more frightening thought could possibly be imagined than that? "It is a fearful thing to fall into the hands of the living God" (Heb 10.31). Therefore, we must each discipline ourselves from continually wandering off the path of holiness in pursuit of our own desires. If we are ever to make our calling and election sure, we must relentlessly live according to the dictates of the Spirit. If we hope to live in assurance of our salvation, war must be declared against our fleshly affections. If we wish to be certain of our place in the ranks of the King, self must be obliterated as the dominant principle of life.

I Cannot Be Selfish and Faithfully Follow Christ

The greatest tragedy of life strikes in the journey of every human being as Satan is allowed to conceal the good news of Jesus with the veil of self-will. Paul grieved over this fact as he wrote, "If our gospel is veiled, it is veiled only to those who are perishing. In their case the god of this world has blinded the minds of the unbelievers, to keep them from seeing the light of the gospel of the glory of Christ, who is the image of God" (2 Cor 4.3–4).

The power of God's word for salvation is lost on human hearts when selfishness reigns. Of all the power exhibited throughout the history of the world, from the greatest of kings to the strongest of empires, no kingdom has gripped and terrorized human destiny like the kingdom of self. The might of ancient Rome pales in comparison. The potency of the United States is a drop in the bucket. All of the kingdoms in all of the world don't form a bastion against righteousness like the kingdom of self. Accordingly, the apostle pleaded with disciples to recognize their higher calling. "We all, with unveiled face, beholding the glory of the Lord, are being transformed into the same image from one degree of glory to another. For this comes from the Lord who is the Spirit" (2 Cor 3.18).

Through the power of Jesus' sacrifice and the Spirit's revelation, I can lift the veil that separates me from my Creator. As I live in harmony with the will of my King, I can put to death the deeds of the body and cling closely to the promises of life. With death to self comes transformation—a shift from conformity with the whims of fallen humanity to submission with the Divine. With transformation comes glory—inexpressible joy over the fact that I am living as God's child, just as God envisioned, to his glory.

But if I submit to the passions and desires of the flesh, a different form of death has been promised. Spiritual death. Separation from the Root of my existence. Self is gratified for the moment, but the most important element of my being—the image of God in my life—dies. As long as I continue to revel in materialism, idolatry, sinful pleasures, selfish ambitions and hypocrisy, the veil between my mind and God's redeeming truth grows only thicker. "Since we have these promises, beloved, let us cleanse ourselves from every defilement of body and spirit, bringing holiness to completion in the fear of God" (2 Cor 7.1).

The battle line is drawn right through the middle of my heart. Someone will occupy the throne of my spirit, but whom? In selfishness I can claim the throne as my own and live in whatever way I choose. I can give lip-service to Jehovah as King, but continue to usurp the throne that rightfully belongs to him as Creator. I can offer prayers to him as Lord, but consistently exalt myself. I can sing of his majesty, but persist to trumpet my own self-centered agenda.

Selfishness is a defilement of the image God intends me to bear. It manifests itself every day in the way image-bearers use their God-given bodies to gratify their own impulses. The Spirit of God cries out through Paul,

> Do you not know that in a race all the runners compete, but only one receives the prize? So run that you may obtain it. Every athlete exercises self-control in all things. They do it to receive a perishable wreath, but we an imperishable. So I do not run aimlessly; I do not box as one beating the air. But I discipline my body and keep it under control, lest after preaching to others I myself should be disqualified. (1 Cor 9.24–27)

Men of integrity must ask themselves, will I control my body, or will I be controlled by my body? There are a great many things in life we cannot control. None of us controls into which family we will be born. The past is beyond our ability to alter and the future is beyond our power to foresee. Each new day brings new circumstances over which we have little sway. For the most part, we cannot control which temptations we will encounter each week. Many of us have trouble controlling our own pets, much less the people around us. So much is outside of our capacity to control.

But there is one thing I must control. Here is one truth I cannot ignore: I must control me. You can control you. Our holy Creator has defined the pathway whereby he might declare fallible human beings as holy. His Spirit invites, "As obedient children, do not be conformed to the passions of your former ignorance, but as he who called you is holy, you also be holy in all your conduct, since it is written, 'You shall be holy, for I am holy'" (1 Pet 1.14–16).

The gate of God's holiness is narrow. My ego won't fit through it. The way is hard that leads to life. If I am determined to try my hand at balancing godliness and self-centeredness, I am doomed to fall. I will never bring the holiness of God to completion in my life without discipline. I will never reach the summit of God's holy mountain if I never place the reins on self.

I cannot be selfish and faithfully follow Christ.

I Cannot Be Selfish and Fully Submit to God's Revelation

How easy it is to read God's revelation through the lenses of self-will! As our eyes pass over the demanding teachings of Jesus, our minds seem naturally to wander to those who need to be rebuked by his message. As our fingers trace a path through Paul's reasoned arguments, we spontaneously wonder how so many people could get it all so wrong. It is self-will that so cleverly and deceptively disguises the logs in our own eyes as we marvel at the specks in the eyes of our neighbors.

When we approach the Scriptures while continuing to wear the lenses of self-will, there is no mystery as to the outcome. Self will be protected at all costs. I will see what I want to see. I will hear what I want to hear. I will rejoice in that which is affirming and I will squirm my way out of that which is condemning. I will exult in that which is pleasant and twist that which demands too much. I will ignore. I will dismiss. I will argue that it doesn't apply. Whatever the cost, self will be justified. Such is the ancient and well-traveled pathway of rationalistic rebellion.

"That a notable sign had been performed" through Peter and John was evident "to all the inhabitants of Jerusalem" in Acts 4.16. The Jewish authorities could not deny it. And yet, they judged these men who had been with Jesus through the lenses of self-will and it led them to reason, "in order that it may spread no further among the people, let us warn them to speak no more to anyone in this name" (Acts 4.17). A miracle had been performed in their midst, but self-will demanded that uncomfortable truths be twisted, dismissed or ignored, regardless of the consequences.

Stephen, full of grace and power, proclaimed Jesus as the Messiah and those who heard him "could not withstand the wisdom and the Spirit with which he was speaking" (Acts 6.10). His bold stand for truth before the high priest and elders of the people is legendary. But as his audience listened and processed his message through the filter of self-will, their reaction was to cry out with a loud voice, stop their ears, and rush together at Stephen. "Then they cast him out of the city and stoned him" (Acts 7.57–58). Self-will always demands personal protection—even violent aggression—whatever the cost. If the messenger must be killed to maintain the citadel of self, so be it.

Paul could stand in a synagogue where the Law and the Prophets were read every Sabbath and be soundly rejected at best, beaten within an inch of his life at worst. Hear his plea:

> "For those who live in Jerusalem and their rulers, because they did not recognize him nor understand the utterances of the prophets, which are read every Sabbath, fulfilled them by condemning him. And though they found in him no guilt worthy of death, they asked Pilate to have him executed." (Acts 13.27–28)

How? Why? Self-will always finds a way to justify rebellion. Ego imposes the blinders necessary to weather the uncomfortable assaults of truth. Though prophecy may find its consummation in my rejection, self-centeredness maintains that the awful price is worthy. And all that is left? The continued fulfillment of Jesus' warning:

> "Seeing they do not see, and hearing they do not hear, nor do they understand. Indeed in their case the prophecy of Isaiah is fulfilled that says:
>
> 'You will indeed hear but never understand,
>   and you will indeed see but never perceive.
> For this people's heart has grown dull,
>   and with their ears they can barely hear,
>   and their eyes they have closed,
>   lest they should see with their eyes
>   and hear with their ears
>   and understand with their heart
>   and turn, and I would heal them.'" (Matt 13.13–15)

When self is allowed to reign, even the edicts of Scripture will be manipulated to preserve my place on the throne. If my present course is condemned, my upbringing threatened, my traditions endangered, my feelings injured, or my convenience jeopardized, self-will demands that truth be struck down.

I cannot be selfish and fully submit to God's revelation.

I Cannot Be Selfish and Treat Others as More Important than Myself

Paul's inspired instructions are simple and straightforward. They are based upon the encouragement we have received in Christ, the comfort we enjoy from his love, and the participation we share with the Spirit. With our aim centered on affection and sympathy, we are exhorted to be "of the same mind, having the same love, being in full accord and of one mind" (Phil 2.1–2). Not once, but twice in the same sentence the divine expectation is reinforced—disciples of Jesus must discipline themselves to be of the same mind.

But how? How can compulsively selfish people of differing backgrounds, cultures, opinions and aspirations possibly operate as if there were a single mind directing them?

Do nothing from rivalry or conceit, but in humility count others more significant than yourselves. Let each of you look not only to his own interests, but also to the interests of others. Have this mind among yourselves, which is yours in Christ Jesus, who, though he was in the form of God, did not count equality with God a thing to be grasped, but made himself nothing, taking the form of a servant, being born in the likeness of men. And being found in human form, he humbled himself by becoming obedient to the point of death, even death on a cross. (Phil 2.3–8)

Leo Tolstoy is attributed as saying, "Everybody thinks of changing humanity and nobody thinks of changing himself." You want to step up. You want to be a leader. You want to make a difference. Otherwise, you wouldn't still be reading this book. But before you dream of having a positive impact on the people and circumstances around you, you must put self into the proper perspective.

"Let love be genuine. Abhor what is evil; hold fast to what is good. Love one another with brotherly affection. Outdo one another in showing honor" (Rom 12.9–10). If you want to journey through life with a feeling of perpetual emptiness, function with complete disregard for the people around you. Let others know just how full of yourself you really are. Outdo them to make yourself look better, and enjoy the nagging void that results, because that will be all that is left.

On the other hand is the call to outdo others in the showing of honor and to recognize that mercy is more satisfying than selfishness. If you wish to enjoy divine fulfillment and purpose, be full of good works for others. In humility count them, their opinions and their dreams as more significant than your own. Realize, however, that only the man who has annihilated self as the dominant principle of life can truly travel that pathway. The *"one another"* markers along the trail are everywhere.

Live in harmony with *one another*. Do not be haughty, but associate with the lowly. Never be conceited. (Rom 12.16)

Therefore welcome *one another* as Christ has welcomed you, for the glory of God. (Rom 15.7)

God has so composed the body, giving greater honor to the part that lacked it, that there may be no division in the body, but that the members may have the same care for *one another*. If one member suffers, all suffer together; if one member is honored, all rejoice together. (1 Cor 12.24–26)

Finally, brothers, rejoice. Aim for restoration, comfort *one another*, agree with *one another*, live in peace; and the God of love and peace will be with you. (2 Cor 13.11)

For you were called to freedom, brothers. Only do not use your freedom as an opportunity for the flesh, but through love serve *one another*. (Gal 5.13)

Brothers, if anyone is caught in any transgression, you who are spiritual should restore him in a spirit of gentleness. Keep watch on yourself, lest you too be tempted. Bear *one another's* burdens, and so fulfill the law of Christ. (Gal 6.1–2)

Be kind to *one another*, tenderhearted, forgiving *one another*, as God in Christ forgave you. (Eph 4.32)

Do not get drunk with wine, for that is debauchery, but be filled with the Spirit, addressing *one another* in psalms and hymns and spiritual songs, singing and making melody to the Lord with your heart, giving thanks always and for everything to God the Father in the name of our Lord Jesus Christ, submitting to *one another* out of reverence for Christ. (Eph 5.18–21)

Put on then, as God's chosen ones, holy and beloved, compassion, kindness, humility, meekness, and patience, bearing with *one another* and, if one has a complaint against another, forgiving each other; as the Lord has forgiven you, so you also must forgive. (Col 3.12–13)

Therefore encourage *one another* and build *one another* up, just as you are doing. (1 Thes 5.11)

See that no one repays anyone evil for evil, but always seek to do good to *one another* and to everyone. (1 Thes 5.15)

Exhort *one another* every day, as long as it is called "today," that none of you may be hardened by the deceitfulness of sin. (Heb 3.13)

Let us consider how to stir up *one another* to love and good works, not neglecting to meet together, as is the habit of some, but encouraging *one another,* and all the more as you see the Day drawing near. (Heb 10.24–25)

Confess your sins to *one another* and pray for *one another,* that you may be healed. (Jas 5.16)

Show hospitality to *one another* without grumbling. As each has received a gift, use it to serve *one another,* as good stewards of God's varied grace. (1 Pet 4.9–10)

The Spirit's message? That's simple. It's time to stop living for myself! It's not about me. The world doesn't revolve around me. I'm simply a steward and it's time I started acting like it.

I cannot be selfish and treat others as more important than myself.

I Cannot Be Selfish and Serve as a Godly Leader

Husbands and fathers have not only been called by the Creator to zealously watch over their own souls, but to serve as the platoon leaders of their families. Read the Spirit's instructions and grasp how selfishness on the part of the leader is akin to dropping a grenade into your own bunker.

Husbands, love your wives, as Christ loved the church and gave himself up for her, that he might sanctify her, having cleansed her by the washing of water with the word, so that he might present the church to himself in splendor, without spot or wrinkle or any such thing, that she might be holy and without blemish. In the same way husbands should love their wives as their own bodies. He who loves his wife loves himself. (Eph 5.25–28)

Our Adversary is on the prowl. His first waves of attack often come in the form of discouragement and distraction. He loves to sow the seeds of resentment in willing hearts. Carelessly give in and he can use you to destroy your own marriage. He can manipulate your self-centeredness and demolish your closest relationship. He can pervert your ego and obliterate years worth of trust and commitment. The godly soldier's primary line of defense is committing every single day to loving his wife as his own body and vowing to cherish her as he cherishes himself.

"Fathers, do not provoke your children to anger, but bring them up in the discipline and instruction of the Lord" (Eph 6.4). As long as self is exalted as the dominant principle in life, this divine mandate for fathers will never be met as God proposed. If personal convenience comes out on top of every circumstance, a father will never be the self-sacrificing leader the Father envisioned. When daddy-time never wins out over down-time, a man may be biologically responsible for his child, yet fail to be the nurturer our Creator intended.

The inconvenient truth is that children are, by nature, inconvenient at times. They wake up in the middle of the night. They demand attention when fathers are busy. As they grow, there are practices to attend, recitals to hear, games to watch, fundraisers to work and friends to pick up. Children require money. Lots of money. They require time. Your time.

When you bring a child into this world, you've signed on to do those inconvenient things which are necessary to help that child develop as a friend, a student, a worker and a citizen. Of greatest significance, of course, is bringing that child up in the discipline and instruction of the Lord. As the parent of that child, you are responsible for raising him or her to become a child of God. It falls upon you to lead your family in opportunities to study God's word. You are called upon to be the primary example of prayer, discipline, brotherly concern and sincere devotion.

In Matthew 16.26 Jesus asked, "For what will it profit a man if he gains the whole world and forfeits his soul? Or what will a man give in exchange for his soul?" The same applies for the souls of that man's children. What job promotion, what ballgame, what boat, what computer, what movie is worth the soul of your child? Fail your children because of your own self-centeredness and you will have failed your Father.

I cannot be selfish and serve as a godly leader.

Conclusion

Think about the ground we've covered—our relationship with God, our response to his word, our interaction with others and our responsibility to our families. Look in the mirror and stare into the one who singlehandedly has the power to destroy it all! Jesus died so that you might no longer live for yourself. He endured the cross so that I could relinquish control and allow him to live in and through me. Even if he is never allowed to reign in the heart of another human being, he is reigning in heaven. As the King of kings and Lord of lords he commands,

> "You shall love the Lord your God with all your heart and with all your soul and with all your mind. This is the great and first commandment. And a second is like it: You shall love your neighbor as yourself. On these two commandments depend all the Law and the Prophets." (Matt 22.37–40)

Are we listening?

6

Sexual Immorality

Learning When to Fight and When to Run

> Or do you not know that your body is a temple of the Holy Spirit within you, whom you have from God? You are not your own, for you were bought with a price. So glorify God in your body. (1 Cor 6.19–20)

I was floored by a recent discussion with six other Christian guys in their twenties and thirties. Our group was studying God's warnings against sexual immorality and instructions for mental and physical purity. After reading from a variety of texts in both the Old and New Testaments, our discussion naturally turned to past experiences. Over the course of the next two hours, it came out that each of those six young guys had been flirted with or propositioned in one way or another by women other than their wives. When did it occur in each instance? While the young men were at work—away from other Christians, away from their homes, and away from their wives.

In a world where nearly all shades of infidelity are viewed as "the norm" for any typical guy, the man of integrity must grow to be armed and ready to meet and defeat the temptations of sexual immorality. Remember our encouragement: "Since we are surrounded by so great a cloud of witnesses, let us also lay aside every weight, and sin which clings so closely, and let us run with endurance the race that is set before us" (Heb 12.1).

One of those "witnesses" who has already run this part of every man's race and passed through the many obstacles successfully is Joseph. As a vital part of our Boot Camp training, let's spend some time in his classroom.

The Scene Of The Temptation

Genesis 39.6 sets the scene effectively for us: "Now Joseph was handsome in form and appearance." Remember, Joseph is hundreds of miles away from home at this point, having been sold by his own brothers as a worthless slave. Whatever he does in this distant land, odds are, not one member of his family will ever find out. He's not married. That means he's free, right? Free to do whatever he wants. After all, who will ever know or even care anyway, especially when we remember the position Joseph now occupies in the house of a man named Potiphar, the captain of Pharaoh's guard.

> Joseph found favor in [Potiphar's] sight and attended him, and [Potiphar] made him overseer of his house and put him in charge of all that he had. …So he left all that he had in Joseph's charge, and because of him he had no concern about anything but the food he ate. (Gen 39.4, 6)

Talk about freedom! Joseph's got boat loads. In many respects, he's his own boss. He can function at this point in relative obscurity and ease. It would certainly have been easy to believe that there were finally nothing but blue skies and smooth waters ahead. And if anyone deserved the benefits and luxuries that came with the package, it was clearly Joseph.

It would not be long, however, before temptation reared its alluring head and Joseph would find himself in the midst of a serious battle. "After a time his master's wife cast her eyes on Joseph and said, 'Lie with me'" (Gen 39.7). There it is—an open, seductively-engraved invitation. As a man, can't you hear the seeds of fantasy and rationalization that would quite naturally bounce around within your mind? "Who will ever know? What will it hurt? I deserve this. She's the one who approached me. It's not that big of a deal. Just this once. I won't let it go too far."

In your mind, picture our Drill Instructor for the Sexual Immorality 101 course of Boot Camp. Joseph has been there. He's a veteran of those battles. He bears the scars to prove it. He spent more than two years as a prisoner of the war of integrity—two years lost because of his valiant fight as a soldier of character.

Does he have your attention? As he looks you in the eye as few men ever have, his question for you is as simple as it is straightforward. "Do you want to be a man of integrity? Do you want to run the race set before you with honor and dignity?"

If so, like Joseph, you've got to be armed and ready when a temptation of this sort blindsides you. He encourages you to learn from his tough experiences. He's here to show you how the Adversary works and where he could strike at any moment. And nothing would please this seasoned veteran of the struggle for godliness more than to equip us so that we can fight and win just as he did.

Someone tentatively raises their hand and asks our instructor, "What was the secret to your success?" Now that's a good question.

"My Mind Is Already Made Up"

Here's the first rule of engagement for every soldier of integrity. Genesis 39.8 tells us that Joseph "refused." How did he come through the battle successfully? His mind had already been made up. The answer was "no." Later that same day, the answer would be "no." The answer would be "no" tomorrow. As far as Joseph was concerned, it was always going to be "no."

Remember what we said in Chapter 4 about mixing standards? Joseph stands tall in God's great cloud of witnesses as a model of sincerity. With his whole heart he had already made up his mind. He wasn't going to allow himself the luxury of conflicting standards. He wouldn't give in to the temptations to reason, "I'll say 'no' for now, but 'maybe' later. I'll say 'no' to going all the way, but 'yes' to something a little more innocent. I'll say 'no' to this woman, but who knows about the next?"

Listen to Joseph! If you and I have any hope of surviving and ultimately winning the war for our souls, here is a lesson we must learn. Make up your mind right now! Dare to stand like Joshua, having chosen beforehand whom you will serve (Josh 24.15). Make up your mind as to what you will and will not do before the temptation hits.

That's what Job did when it came to sexual temptation. "I have made a covenant with my eyes," he said in Job 31.1; "how then could I gaze at a virgin?" To paraphrase, Job's mindset was,

> My eyes and I have already sat down and discussed the issue. We've come to an agreement. We're already on the same page. Through the course of the day, I may happen to see a lovely young lady, but I will not take the opportunity to gaze at her. I refuse to allow myself the luxury of making up my mind on a case-by-case, woman-by-woman basis. My eyes and my mind already understand what is and is not appropriate. The answer is "NO!"

Why take such a hard and fast stand? Remember, Job had been richly blessed with material goods. "He possessed 7,000 sheep, 3,000 camels, 500 yoke of oxen, and 500 female donkeys, and very many servants, so that this man was the greatest of all the people of the east" (Job 1.3). Job was in a position to enjoy whatever his heart could desire. But he was also humble and honest enough to recognize the consequences of giving in to sexual immorality.

> "What would be my portion from God above
>   and my heritage from the Almighty on high?
> Is not calamity for the unrighteous,
>   and disaster for the workers of iniquity?
> Does not he see my ways
>   and number all my steps?" (Job 31.2–4)

In other words, "Even though I have bountiful physical blessings, what can I expect from my Father if I'm not a man of godly character?" Rather, "Let me be weighed in a just balance, and let God know my integrity!" (Job 31.6). "My mind is already made up!"

Is yours? Is your answer already "no"?

"Some Things Don't Belong To Me"

Here's the second line of defense for the soldier of the cross. What can you say when approached in some inappropriate way by a member of the opposite sex? She makes it obvious that you've caught her attention. She grows progressively more bold in her flirting. She "suddenly" shows up at very awkward times and seems to enjoy the awkwardness. She's relentless. She begins to push the limits. You never know when the next confrontation could come and you begin to dread the very thought of the possibilities.

Welcome to Joseph's world. Potiphar's wife "spoke to Joseph day after day," tempting him "to lie beside her or to be with her" (Gen 39.10). Notice carefully her tactics. They are significant because they perfectly illustrate the "mixing standards" point of Chapter 4. Unable to persuade him to yield in her initial attempts, Potiphar's wife decides to assault Joseph with the temptation to compromise. "If you won't be with me, at least lie beside me."

Have you ever been tempted in that way? With seemingly innocent, little steps? Nothing too dramatic. "We won't go all the way. We won't actually have intercourse. It's just a little kiss. It's nothing more than a brush of skin on skin. What's the harm in just making out? What will it hurt if we just take off our clothes and lie beside each other? Is oral sex really that big of a deal?"

While some of my older readers may be quite uncomfortable at this point, I can assure you that many of my younger readers aren't even blushing yet.[1] Men, it's time that we got to the heart of the matter. The temptation to compromise is real. It's powerful. It's deadly. I may enter into a confrontation with the determination to refuse, but I quickly reach the point where I must say something. What will it be? Words of integrity and strength, or words of compromise?

How did Joseph handle this volatile situation? We know "he refused," but what did he actually say?

> "Behold, because of me my master has no concern about anything in the house, and he has put everything that he has in my charge. He is not greater in this house than I am, nor has he kept back anything from me except yourself, because you are his wife." (Gen 39.8–9)

Take the time to appreciate Joseph's inner strength. He's not a man who doubts himself. He knows who he is, and he's not ashamed of it. Some men naturally morph into the equivalent of a third grader when tempted by a seductive woman. Not Joseph. In the midst of a tantalizing struggle, we get the impression that he speaks with authority.

But notice also Joseph's sense of moral balance. "Am I important? Yes! Have I been given great responsibilities? Absolutely. Are there a number of perks that come with my position? Without a doubt. Does that mean I can do whatever I want? Not for a moment!"

"Nor has he kept back anything from me except yourself, because you are his wife" (Gen 39.9). Men, it's time to listen, and listen carefully to our instructor in this part of the Boot Camp of integrity. The fact that you've been blessed with eyes doesn't mean you have the right to look. The fact that you've been blessed with feet doesn't mean you have the right to go wherever you want. The fact that God has created you as a male to naturally yearn for a physical relationship with a female doesn't mean you have the right to act in whatever way you desire. There are some things that don't belong to you!

You don't have the right to a married woman other than your wife. Joseph realized that. The only person on the face of the earth who had any kind of sexual rights to that woman was Potiphar, her husband. "Let marriage be held in honor among all, and let the marriage bed be undefiled, for God will judge the sexually immoral and adulterous" (Heb 13.4). If a woman is married, she is off-limits. Period.

You don't have the right to a single woman. Just because both parties aren't married doesn't mean they're free to act in whatever way their fleshly passions dictate. Sex with a married person is referred to as *adultery,* but the Bible also condemns sex between unmarried people as *fornication* or *sexual immorality.* Notice how inappropriate sexual behavior tops the cautionary list on several New Testament occasions:

Now the works of the flesh are evident: sexual immorality, impurity, sensuality, idolatry, sorcery, enmity, strife, jealousy, fits of anger, rivalries, dissensions, divisions, envy, drunkenness, orgies, and things like these. I warn you, as I warned you before, that those who do such things will not inherit the kingdom of God. (Gal 5.19–21)

Put to death therefore what is earthly in you: sexual immorality, impurity, passion, evil desire, and covetousness, which is idolatry. On account of these the wrath of God is coming. (Col 3.5–6)

For this is the will of God, your sanctification: that you abstain from sexual immorality; that each one of you know how to control his own body in holiness and honor, not in the passion of lust like the Gentiles who do not know God. (1 Thes 4.3–5)

Is the woman in whom you're interested still single? Wonderful! Just remember that you don't have a sexual right to her until you marry her. Period.

*You don't have the right to sexually fantasize about **any** woman who is not your wife.* What did Jesus say about the "Look-just-as-long-as-you-don't-touch" way of approaching things?

"You have heard that it was said, 'You shall not commit adultery.' But I say to you that everyone who looks at a woman with lustful intent, has already committed adultery with her in his heart." (Matt 5.27–28)

Remember, just because you've been blessed with eyes doesn't mean you have the right to look. If you look at any woman other than your wife with lust in your heart, you've sinned. Period.

Listen to our Drill Instructor. The battle is raging all around us! As soldiers of the cross, now is the time to clearly define the boundaries and to recognize that some things just don't belong to us. We live in a world of traps and temptations on every hand. The examples of those in the high places of our society who have compromised their values in this regard are innumerable. Tragically, even those who have been a part of the Lord's church for decades are not immune. The battle comes to our doorstep daily.

Let me challenge you, as a man seeking the integrity of God, to take the wise message of Proverbs 5.15–23 to heart.

Drink water from your own cistern,
> flowing water from your own well.
Should your springs be scattered abroad,
> streams of water in the streets?
Let them be for yourself alone,
> and not for strangers with you.
Let your fountain be blessed,
> and rejoice in the wife of your youth,
> a lovely deer, a graceful doe.
Let her breasts fill you at all times with delight;
> be intoxicated always in her love.
Why should you be intoxicated,
> my son, with a forbidden woman
> and embrace the bosom of an adulteress?
For a man's ways are before the eyes of the LORD,
> and he ponders all his paths.
The iniquities of the wicked ensnare him,
> and he is held fast in the cords of sin.
He dies for lack of discipline,
> and because of his great folly he is led astray.

The sexual relationship enjoyed by a man and woman is a beautiful thing. To demonize it is to disparage a divinely created and sanctioned joy of human existence. But the man who does not realize and respect the fact that our Creator has regulated the joys associated with sex is a fool skipping along the pathway to hell. Sex as God envisioned always involves one man and one woman within the bonds of marriage.

"This Is a Sin Against God"

"How then can I do this great wickedness and sin against God?" (Gen 39.9). There's our third rule of engagement. Remember, Joseph is hundreds of miles away from home. His father would never find out about his indiscretion. In his current position, he could arrange the circumstances so that no one would find out. And if no one finds out, what's the big deal?

Let's allow David, a man who learned this timeless truth the hard way, to answer that question for all time.

O LORD, you have searched me and known me!
You know when I sit down and when I rise up;
    you discern my thoughts from afar.
You search out my path and my lying down
    and are acquainted with all my ways.
Even before a word is on my tongue,
    behold, O LORD, you know it altogether.
You hem me in, behind and before,
    and lay your hand upon me.
Such knowledge is too wonderful for me;
    it is high; I cannot attain it.
Where shall I go from your Spirit?
    Or where shall I flee from your presence?
If I ascend to heaven, you are there!
    If I make my bed in Sheol, you are there!
If I take the wings of the morning
    and dwell in the uttermost parts of the sea,
Even there your hand shall lead me,
    and your right hand shall hold me.
If I say, "Surely the darkness shall cover me,
    and the light about me be night,"
Even the darkness is not dark to you;
    the night is bright as the day,
    for darkness is as light with you. (Psa 139.1–12)

You can't afford to overlook or forget this third rule of engagement in Sexual Immorality 101. As you step on the deadly land mines of fornication or adultery, it not only affects you and the person with whom you sin, it's an affront to the Almighty himself who knows exactly what you've done.

Long ago, the prophet Habakkuk affirmed the fact that our Lord is "of purer eyes than to see evil and cannot look at wrong" (Hab 1.13). It makes him nauseated. God is the forgiving Father of the "prodigal son" who selfishly demands his portion of the family inheritance, travels into a far country and wastes all of his blessings on wild living, allowing his father's heritage to be "devoured with prostitutes" (Luke 15.11–32). Our holy Creator graciously enables rebellious human beings who have mocked and spat in his Son's face to overcome their slavery to corruption. As Peter wrote, "The Lord is not slow to fulfill his promise as some count slowness, but is patient toward you, not wishing that any should perish, but that all should reach repentance" (2 Pet 3.9).

Far too often, however, our Father is forced to watch as one of his own, having "escaped the defilements of the world," becomes "again entangled in them and overcome." How does this make him feel?

> The last state has become worse for them than the first. For it would have been better for them never to have known the way of righteousness than after knowing it to turn back from the holy commandment delivered to them. What the true proverb says has happened to them: "The dog returns to its own vomit, and the sow, after washing herself, returns to wallow in the mire." (2 Pet 2.20–22)

Jehovah is "of purer eyes than to see evil and cannot look at wrong," but he can see us perfectly as we wallow in our sin-soaked filthiness. Those were the cold, hard facts that David had to come to grips with after his night of adultery with Bathsheba:

> For I know my transgressions,
> and my sin is ever before me.
> Against you, you only, have I sinned
> and done what is evil in your sight. (Psa 51.3–4)

This is why we are repeatedly warned throughout the New Testament:

> The body is not meant for sexual immorality, but for the Lord, and the Lord for the body. (1 Cor 6.13)

> But among you there must not be even a hint of sexual immorality, or of any kind of impurity, or of greed, because these are improper for God's holy people. (Eph 5.3, NIV)

> Therefore, since Christ suffered in his body, arm yourselves also with the same attitude, because he who has suffered in his body is done with sin. As a result, he does not live the rest of his

earthly life for evil human desires, but rather for the will of God. For you have spent enough time in the past doing what pagans choose to do—living in debauchery, lust, drunkenness, orgies, carousing and detestable idolatry. (1 Pet 4.1–3, NIV)

Our bodies are meant to be used for the glory of our Creator. Sexual immorality, lust, and impurity are improper for the holy people whom the Father sacrificed so greatly to redeem. If I were blessed with 10,000 lifetimes, I deserve nothing more than to selflessly give the rest of my existence completely over to the will of God.

> Love so amazing, so divine,
>> Demands my soul, my life, my all. (Isaac Watts)

Listen soberly to Joseph. You can't hide from the Almighty. He sees. He knows. Whether you're the overseer of a rich man's house in Egypt, or in the backseat of a car with your date on Friday night, or working overtime in a dark office with no one but your secretary, or in a lonely hotel room miles away from home, God sees. God knows.

"Sometimes the Bravest Thing You Can Do Is Run"

But one day, when he went into the house to do his work and none of the men of the house was there in the house, she caught him by his garment, saying, "Lie with me." (Gen 39.11–12)

The great struggle between the lusts of the flesh and honorable integrity had reached its climax. No one else was in the house. Potiphar's wife had lost her patience. She intended to take what she wanted, and take it at that very moment. She physically grabbed hold of Joseph, "but he left his garment in her hand and fled and got out of the house" (Gen 39.11–12).

We don't generally commend soldiers for their strength and courage when they run away as the battle reaches its boiling point, but this is a different kind of battle against a different kind of Enemy. Remember, "We do not wrestle against flesh and blood, but against the rulers, against the authorities, against the cosmic powers over this present darkness, against the spiritual forces of evil in the heavenly places" (Eph 6.12).

The last rule of engagement in Sexual Immorality 101 is this: sometimes the bravest thing you can do is run. Isn't that what Paul was trying to convey in 1 Corinthians 6.18 when he wrote, "Flee from sexual immorality. Every other sin a person commits is outside the body, but the sexually immoral person sins against his own body." It's worth noting that the word we have translated *flee* is *pheugo* in Greek, a verb in the present tense that implies a constant, habitual running away. "Run away from sexual sin! Always run! And keep running as you run! Don't look back!"

Don't forget this last point from Joseph's powerful example. Some of the land mines we run across on the battlefield for our souls are most effectively defeated by constant opposition and persistent fighting. But let's face it. The Lord's battle plan against the deadly traps of sexual immorality calls for holy retreat.

Is your secretary getting a little too close? "Do not desire her beauty in your heart, and do not let her capture you with her eyelashes" (Prov 6.25).

Is your Friday night date wanting to go farther than you know is appropriate? "Can a man carry fire next to his chest and his clothes not be burned?" (Prov 6.27).

Have you run across a dark treasure chest of sinful images online? "For the lips of a forbidden woman drip honey, and her speech is smoother than oil, but in the end she is bitter as wormwood, sharp as a two-edged sword" (Prov 5.3–4).

Is your next door neighbor doing everything she can to get your inappropriate attention? "Can one walk on hot coals and his feet not be scorched? So is he who goes in to his neighbor's wife; none who touches her will go unpunished" (Prov 6.28–29).

Does the lonely hotel room seem like it provides the perfect opportunity? "The eyes of the Lord are in every place, keeping watch on the evil and the good" (Prov 15.3).

Are the circumstances around you piling up to the point that you're not sure you can control yourself? "Flee youthful passions" (2 Tim 2.22).

Are you already in bondage to sinful sexual habits and rationalizing that it's not that big of a deal? "Do not be deceived: God is not mocked, for whatever one sows, that will he also reap. For the one who sows to his own flesh will from the flesh reap corruption, but the one who sows to the Spirit will from the Spirit reap eternal life" (Gal 6.7–8).

The rallying cry for this part of the war for your soul was delivered by Paul in Romans 13.13–14:

> Let us cast off the works of darkness and put on the armor of light. Let us walk properly as in the daytime, not in orgies and drunkenness, not in sexual immorality and sensuality, not in quarreling and jealousy. But put on the Lord Jesus Christ, and make no provision for the flesh to gratify its desires.

The great day of God is coming. On that day, you and I will stand before the same throne as Joseph and "God will bring every deed into judgment, with every secret thing, whether good or evil" (Ecc 12.14). Because of his steadfast integrity and courageous character, Joseph will be ready to stand. Will you?

7

Idolatry

To What am I Pledging My Allegiance?

> If we had forgotten the name of our God or extended our hands
> to a strange god, would not God find this out? For He knows the
> secrets of the heart. (Psa 44.20–21, NASB)

As we move from Sexual Immorality 101 to Idolatry 101 in our
Boot Camp experience, we find three new instructors waiting for
us. Their names are Hananiah, Mishael and Azariah. Of course,
you may not recognize their Hebrew names. We're generally more
familiar with their Chaldean names: Shadrach, Meshach and
Abednego. They welcome us into their classroom and encourage
us to listen carefully.

To begin, they remind us of one of our most basic rules of engagement from the last chapter—make up your mind before the
temptation hits. These young men are another perfect illustration
of that survival skill. Like Joseph, they also found themselves far
away from home, in a strange land, with challenging decisions to
make in the heat of the moment. Like us, their decisions would
affect their destiny. The value of our time in their classroom,
therefore, cannot be overemphasized.

They take us back to 605 BC:

> In the third year of the reign of Jehoiakim king of Judah, Nebu-
> chadnezzar king of Babylon came to Jerusalem and besieged it.
> And the Lord gave Jehoiakim king of Judah into his hand, with

some of the vessels of the house of God. And he brought them to the land of Shinar, to the house of his god, and placed the vessels in the treasury of his god. Then the king commanded Ashpenaz, his chief eunuch, to bring some of the people of Israel, both of the royal family and of the nobility, youths without blemish, of good appearance and skillful in all wisdom, endowed with knowledge, understanding learning, and competent to stand in the king's palace, and to teach them the literature and language of the Chaldeans. (Dan 1.1–4)

Hananiah, Mishael and Azariah were among these young men. They were literally uprooted and replanted in a foreign land. Their future consisted of being completely assimilated into the Babylonian culture.

One part of the integration process was the changing of their names—a way to emphasize absolute authority over the youths of Israel. Their Hebrew names testified of Jehovah, the God of their forefathers. *Hananiah* meant "Jehovah has been gracious." *Mishael* asked "Who is what God is?" *Azariah* declared "Jehovah has helped."

But with a new life and new responsibilities came new Babylonian names that honored Chaldean deities. Hananiah was changed to *Shadrach*, "Command of Aku" (the Babylonian moon god). Mishael came to be known as *Meshach*, "Who is what Aku is?" Azariah became *Abednego*, "Servant of Nebo" (the Babylonian god mentioned in Isaiah 46.1).

The obvious question is, would this change in identity lead to a change of allegiance in the young men? Wasn't that the goal of the Babylonians? By altering their names, the chief eunuch of Nebuchadnezzar sought to break their connection with the God of the Jews. The not-so-subtle message was, "Our gods are stronger than your God, otherwise, why would you be our slaves?"

Hundreds of miles away from home, having been educated for three years in the court of the most powerful monarch of the day, how would young Hananiah, Mishael and Azariah respond? The authorities had changed their names, but had the young men evolved in their loyalty? We turn to Daniel 3 and find our answer.

Nebuchadnezzar's Golden Image

King Nebuchadnezzar made an image of gold, whose height was sixty cubits and its breadth six cubits. (Dan 3.1)

Picture it in your mind: a golden statue, some ninety feet tall and nine feet wide. Whether a representation of Nebuchadnezzar himself, a particular god, or simply a symbol of his might and dominion, we're not specifically told. But we do know that it towered high above all the people, and it was to be worshiped.

At its dedication, Nebuchadnezzar's herald proclaimed for all the empire to hear:

"You are commanded, O peoples, nations, and languages, that when you hear the sound of the horn, pipe, lyre, trigon, harp, bagpipe, and every kind of music, you are to fall down and worship the golden image that King Nebuchadnezzar has set up." (Dan 3.4–5)

To the average inhabitant of Babylon, this probably wouldn't be that big of a deal. After all, it was just one more of many objects to which they paid homage. But for the descendant of Abraham, the story was different. Regardless of the three long years of Babylonian education, in spite of their new Chaldean names, words that had been emblazoned on the hearts of these young men would have immediately sprung to mind.

"You shall have no other gods before me. You shall not make for yourself a carved image, or any likeness of anything that is in heaven above, or that is in the earth beneath, or that is in the water under the earth. You shall not bow down to them or serve them, for I the LORD your God am a jealous God." (Exod 20.3–5)

"You shall not make idols for yourselves or erect an image or pillar, and you shall not set up a figured stone in your land to bow down to it, for I am the LORD your God." (Lev 26.1)

"Take care lest your heart be deceived, and you turn aside and serve other gods and worship them; then the anger of the LORD will be kindled against you." (Deut 11.16–17)

The list of Scriptures could go on and on. Israel had been warned of few things more in the Law of Moses than idolatry. But how could these young men possibly fulfill Nebuchadnezzar's clear edict while remaining faithful to the one true God? And on top of it all, Nebuchadnezzar's herald isn't even done delivering the final details of the royal decree. Apparently, opposition had already been anticipated and the motivation of fear is authoritatively provided: "And whoever does not fall down and worship shall immediately be cast into a burning fiery furnace" (Dan 3.6).

Such would be enough to get anyone's attention, and it doesn't take long for the subjects of Nebuchadnezzar to make a decision on their allegiance: "Therefore, as soon as all the peoples heard the sound of the horn, pipe, lyre, trigon, harp, bagpipe, and every kind of music, all the peoples, nations, and languages fell down and worshiped the golden image that King Nebuchadnezzar had set up" (Dan 3.7).

All the people, except three very conspicuous young men. Imagine being Shadrach and hearing the sound of those instruments for the first time. What would it be like for Meshach to watch as everyone around him suddenly began to bow? What would Abednego have been thinking?

And what kind of an impact would it have had on the people who had bowed and suddenly noticed out of the corners of their eyes these three young men standing tall? "What are you doing?" "Didn't you hear?!" These three young Jews may have gotten more than one anxious tug on their garments. The looks they received would have said it all.

But they would not bow.

It wasn't long before certain individuals came before the king and "maliciously accused" the young Jews: "These men, O king, pay no attention to you; they do not serve your gods or worship the golden image that you have set up" (Dan 3.12).

In a furious rage, Nebuchadnezzar commands that Shadrach, Meshach and Abednego be brought before him. As they stand before the most powerful man on the face of the earth, they are asked at point-blank range, "Is it true?"

Before you read any further, do your best to stop and place yourself in that moment.

What will you say?

Once again, it's not hard to imagine how every excuse and word of compromise in the book would suddenly rattle through your head. After all, it's your *life* on the line! And all the more so when the warning is repeated: "If you do not worship, you shall immediately be cast into a burning fiery furnace. And who is the god who will deliver you out of my hands?" (Dan 3.15)

One thing is clear: Nebuchadnezzar means business. Give in and live. Defy and fry.

Remarkably, however, "excuse" isn't in the vocabulary of these young men. "Compromise" doesn't even enter the picture. How? Why? Let's just listen.

> "O Nebuchadnezzar, we have no need to answer you in this matter. If this be so, our God whom we serve is able to deliver us from the burning fiery furnace, and he will deliver us out of your hand, O king. But if not, be it known to you, O king, that we will not serve your gods or worship the golden image that you have set up." (Dan 3.16–18)

What makes these young men special? Come what may, their minds have already been made up. Their allegiance has already been pledged. They are unashamed of their stand. They don't need a second chance. The decision is already final, and their faith is strong. They believe with everything they are that the God of their forefathers will deliver them from Nebuchadnezzar, but even if he does not, they will not budge.

What greater example of strength and fortitude can you find than that? As you and I sit in their classroom and listen to the story being told, one thing is clear. These men were soldiers in the Lord's army. They were warriors of courage and conviction. If they lost their lives for Jehovah's cause, so be it.

Face to Face with the Idols of Our Own Making
At this point in the class, Hananiah, Mishael and Azariah

look at you. What about your life? While they are now a part of that "great cloud of witnesses," your race still very much lies before you. What pressures are you experiencing to "bow down" before the idols of our own day and age?

We've been plainly told that the only "image" worthy of our adoration and allegiance is Jesus. Remember, He "is the image of God" (2 Cor 4.4), "the radiance of the glory of God and the exact imprint of his nature" (Heb 1.3). No image of wood or stone or metal is worthy of our worship. When compared with the one true God, all else is worthless. Anything less than the Almighty is idolatry, and idolatry is sin. Idolatry is defection, and defection is a betrayal of our Creator. "Those who pay regard to vain idols forsake their hope of steadfast love" (Jon 2.8).

But before we blow off idolatry as an Old Testament transgression with no real 21st century relevance, let's make sure we take a moment to notice the New Testament warnings. In Romans 1.24–25, Paul speaks of those given up by God "in the lusts of their hearts to impurity, to the dishonoring of their bodies among themselves, because they exchanged the truth about God for a lie and worshiped and served the creature rather than the Creator." Such sounds like idolatry.

In 1 Corinthians 6.9–10, Paul asks,

> Do you not know that the unrighteous will not inherit the kingdom of God? Do not be deceived: neither the sexually immoral, nor idolaters, nor adulterers, nor men who practice homosexuality, nor thieves, nor the greedy, nor drunkards, nor revilers, nor swindlers will inherit the kingdom of God.

In 1 Corinthians 10.14, the admonition is simple and straightforward: "Therefore, my beloved, flee from idolatry." Once again we've come across a temptation that is most effectively defeated by tactical retreat. In Galatians 5.19–21, idolatry is listed as one of the "works of the flesh" that will hinder men from inheriting "the kingdom of God." In 1 John 5.21, John closes his letter by encouraging, "Little children, keep yourselves from idols." In Revelation 21.7–8, the King who resides on heaven's throne is pictured as saying, "As for the cowardly, the faithless, the detestable, as for murderers, the sexually immoral, sorcerers, idolaters, and all liars, their portion will be in the lake that burns with fire and sulfur, which is the second death."

Revelation 22.15 pictures those outside the gates of the heavenly city as being "the dogs and sorcerers and the sexually immoral and murderers and idolaters, and everyone who loves and practices falsehood."

Disciples of Christ are obviously warned about idolatry as if it were a clear and present danger. Quite evidently, idolatry did not cease to jeopardize the souls of men with the close of the Old Testament. Therefore, the most important question we could ask in this section of Boot Camp is, what forms do the deceptively hidden land mines of idolatry take and where will we find them on the modern battlefield?

Covetousness

The apostle Paul unmistakably connected the deadly dots for us on two different occasions. In Ephesians 5.5, he confidently asserted, "For you may be sure of this, that everyone who is sexually immoral or impure, or who is covetous (that is, an idolater), has no inheritance in the kingdom of Christ and God."

To the saints in Colosse, "Put to death therefore what is earthly in you: sexual immorality, impurity, passion, evil desire, and covetousness, which is idolatry. On account of these the wrath of God is coming" (Col 3.5–6).

What is covetousness? In one word, greed. Greed can become my idol just as surely as Nebuchadnezzar's golden statue was an idol in ancient Babylon. Any time the things of this world come between me and God, I've erected an idol in my life. That's precisely why the gauntlet has already been thrown down by the Son of God himself: "No one can serve two masters, for either he will hate the one and love the other, or he will be devoted to the one and despise the other. You cannot serve God and money" (Matt 6.24).

Of the various weapons our Adversary is successfully using against us in the 21st century, one of the most effective must be the idol of greed. And how many of us are being spiritually blown away on the battlefield for our souls without even realizing it? Who among us could deny that if the apostle Paul was looking over the average American city, his spirit would be "provoked within him as he saw that the city was full of idols" (Acts 17.16)? Houses. Yards. Cars. Boats. Televisions. Video games. Computers. Sports. Hobbies. Luxuries. Things that have been unsuspectingly allowed to come before the Almighty.

In order to get to the heart of the matter, let me ask you four questions. Be honest. Do your best to answer them without excuse or justification.

How many times in the average week do you worry about money and the things that you own?

How much debt are you in?

If you're married, how many arguments with your spouse revolve in one way or another around money and its use?

How much of that worry, how much of that debt, and how many of those arguments have been brought on as a direct result of greed for things that you didn't truly need?

I've never met a young couple who didn't worry about their bank account. Carefree nights where you didn't spend one anxious moment before fading off to sleep have since been replaced with sleepless nights where you wonder how you and your spouse are going to possibly make ends meet. More than ever before, we live in a paycheck-to-paycheck society that consistently spends more than is earned. Our minimum payments easily exceed our maximum budgets and the only way to stay afloat is to continue to "charge it!" We've enslaved ourselves to our "abundant" lifestyles. The peace of God that surpasses all understanding has been effortlessly displaced with the stress of monthly gold card statements that only bury us deeper. And why? Who could dispute that one of the major factors is old fashioned greed?

Both Testaments seek to warn us ahead of time:

Riches do not profit in the day of wrath, but righteousness delivers from death. (Prov 11.4)

He who loves money will not be satisfied with money, nor he who loves wealth with his income; this also is vanity. (Ecc 5.10)

Those who desire to be rich fall into temptation, into a snare, into many senseless and harmful desires that plunge people into ruin and destruction. For the love of money is a root of all kinds of evil. It is through this craving that some have wandered away from the faith and pierced themselves with many pangs. (1 Tim 6.9–10)

The warnings are plain throughout God's Word—idolatry can kill you.

Perhaps the most striking passage of all is found in Paul's first letter to the first-century Corinthian Christians: "But now I am writing to you not to associate with anyone who bears the name of brother if he is guilty of sexual immorality or greed, or is an idolater, reviler, drunkard, or swindler—not even to eat with such a one" (1 Cor 5.11).

Strong words from an inspired apostle. But how many times in 21st century America have you heard of greed being the reason behind a withdrawal of fellowship? Odds are not many, if ever. But who will deny that the land mines lie all around us? Could it be that we're not even looking for them?

Materialism

Greed is the drug which leads to the addiction of materialism. Sit down for one hour in front of the television and pay specific attention to the message of the commercials you see. Isn't the basic substance, "I see, I want. You have, I want. I don't have, I want—so I'll do whatever I have to do to get it"? We're indoctrinated with the pursuit of "the American Dream." We praise the people driven by desire for the things of this world. We attach special significance to those who've realized the aspirations of wealth. Our heroes are those who've conquered all odds and now stand atop the corporate ladder. But does the addiction ever culminate in a fix that lasts?

Let's ask the Preacher, the son of David, king in Jerusalem—a man who gave it the worthiest of shots.

> I made great works. I built houses and planted vineyards for myself. I made myself gardens and parks, and planted in them all kinds of fruit trees. I made myself pools from which to water the forest of growing trees. …I had also great possessions of herds and flocks, more than any who had been before me in Jerusalem. I also gathered for myself silver and gold and the treasure of kings and provinces…whatever my eyes desired I did not keep from them. I kept my heart from no pleasure. …Then I considered all that my hands had done and the toil I had expended in doing it, and behold, all was vanity and a striving after wind. (Ecc 2.4–8, 10–11)

Can material concerns hinder my discipleship? Ask the young rich man who came to Jesus in Matthew 19.16–22.

> And behold, a man came up to him, saying, "Teacher, what good deed must I do to have eternal life?" And he said to him, "Why do you ask me about what is good? There is only one who is good. If you would enter life, keep the commandments." He said to him, "Which ones?" And Jesus said, "You shall not murder, You shall not commit adultery, You shall not steal, You shall not bear false witness, Honor your father and mother, and, You shall love your neighbor as yourself." The young man said to him, "All these I have kept. What do I still lack?" Jesus said to him, "If you would be perfect, go, sell what you possess and give to the poor, and you will have treasure in heaven; and come, follow me." When the young man heard this he went away sorrowful, for he had great possessions.

The point? It's been provided by the Son of God himself.

> "Truly, I say to you, only with difficulty will a rich person enter the kingdom of heaven. Again I tell you, it is easier for a camel to go through the eye of a needle than for a rich person to enter the kingdom of God." (Matt 19.23–24)

Our knee-jerk reaction? "Well, good thing I'm not rich!" But listen carefully. Each soldier in the Lord's army must grasp this point. From the perspective of a first-century Galilean, the average American is rich beyond imagination. What would Peter think of our indoor plumbing and air-conditioning? What would Paul say about our motor vehicles? What would James think of our electronic devices? What would John say about the abundance of food we throw in our trash cans every single day? In so many ways, the average American lives like the Herods and Pilates of the ancient world could never have dreamed!

And yet, so many of us—Christians included—continue to live at the mercy of our selfish and childish impulses. If we want it, we're going to get it, even if we don't have the money. If we see it, we act as if we're unable to say "No," or "I'll wait." If it catches our attention, we want it and we want it now.

Untold millions of young people believe that they deserve in the first year of marriage what their parents worked decades to obtain. Young couples enter life together with the conviction that more things will bring more happiness. Long after the wedding cards stop gracing their mailbox, the credit card offers continue to show up, day after day. And sooner than they know what has happened, this new family with a completely fresh start has been consumed by the allurements and costs of "stuff" for years to come. Has it brought everlasting happiness? "All the toil of man is for his mouth, yet his appetite is not satisfied" (Ecc 6.7). I know. I've been there. I've made the mistakes.

In stark contrast, Paul encourages us to recognize, "There is great gain in godliness with contentment, for we brought nothing into the world, and we cannot take anything out of the world. But if we have food and clothing, with these we will be content" (1 Tim 6.6–8).

And if we missed that one, we've got the message contained in Hebrews 13.5: "Make sure that your character is free from the love of money, being content with what you have; for He Himself has said, "I will never desert you, nor will I ever forsake you" (NASB).

The virtuous man molded after God's intention is willing to say with David,

I will ponder the way that is blameless.
Oh when will you come to me?
I will walk with integrity of heart
within my house;
I will not set before my eyes
anything that is worthless. (Psa 101.2–3)

In all honesty, how much of what fills our houses is absolutely worthless? How much of what really matters is being completely overshadowed by frivolous concerns and pointless pursuits? How has our junk affected the integrity of our hearts? How far have our impulses and the undisciplined willingness to indulge them carried us from the Father?

In Luke 8, Jesus lamented the seeds of the Word of God which fell "among thorns, and the thorns grew up with it and choked it…they are those who hear, but as they go on their way they are choked by the cares and riches and pleasures of life, and their fruit does not mature" (8.7, 14). How desperately we need to apply that message as our car payment thorns prevent us from growing in hospitality, our credit card thorns choke our benevolent maturity, our entertainment thorns clog our capacity to share, and the thorns we chalk up to luxury strangle our ability to selflessly give.

It's not that we don't care, it's that we're choked, just as Jesus foretold.

Busyness

To maintain our houses full of idols, we live lives of unprecedented busyness. Realize that we have more indulgent time than any generation that has ever come before us. It takes us less time to cook, to clean, to travel, and to communicate. Ours is an age of absolute convenience. We can save more time accomplishing the basic tasks of life than any generation before us, and yet we constantly complain as if we had less time than any of them! How many Christians make those complaints? How many of the Lord's soldiers wake up each morning and bow down to the idol of busyness?

Consider the rich fool of Jesus' parable in Luke 12.16–21:

> The land of a rich man produced plentifully, and he thought to himself, "What shall I do, for I have nowhere to store my crops?" And he said, "I will do this: I will tear down my barns and build larger ones, and there I will store all my grain and my goods. And I will say to my soul, 'Soul, you have ample goods laid up for many years; relax, eat, drink, be merry.'" But God said to him, "Fool! This night your soul is required of you, and the things you have prepared, whose will they be?" So is the one who lays up treasure for himself and is not rich toward God.

The point? Again, it's been delivered by the Son of God himself. A vital part of being a soldier in the Lord's army is maintaining strict guard duty on my time and priorities. "Take care, and be on your guard against all covetousness, for one's life does not consist in the abundance of his possessions" (Luke 12.15).

Let's make this principle of integrity crystal clear. The fact that you're busy doesn't mean you're important. The fact that you're busy doesn't mean you're getting much done. The fact that you're busy doesn't mean you're successful. The fact that you're busy doesn't mean you're serving as God intends. "Better is a handful of quietness than two hands full of toil and a striving after wind" (Ecc 4.6). How desperately we need to listen to the Biblical admonitions toward quietness!

Do you honestly think you could ever have as much on your mind or be as hard-pressed to accomplish something as Jesus? We know the answer to that question. And yet, notice the discipline modeled during his ministry: "Immediately he made the disciples get into the boat and go before him to the other side, while he dismissed the crowds. And after he had dismissed the crowds, he went up on the mountain by himself to pray" (Matt 14.22–23).

In Mark 1.35, "rising very early in the morning, while it was still dark, he departed and went out to a desolate place, and there he prayed." Mark 6.30–32 documents,

> The apostles returned to Jesus and told him all that they had done and taught. And he said to them, "Come away by yourselves to a

desolate place and rest a while." For many were coming and going, and they had no leisure even to eat. And they went away in the boat to a desolate place by themselves.

Luke 4.42 continues the theme. "And when it was day, he departed and went into a desolate place." Luke 5.16 tells us "he would withdraw to desolate places and pray." Luke 6.12 records, "In these days, he went out to the mountain to pray, and all night he continued in prayer to God."

What do we learn? If you're too busy to pray, you're bowing down to the idol of busyness. If you're too busy to nurture your relationship with your wife, you're worshiping the idol of busyness. If you're too busy to spend recreational time, Bible study time, and prayer time with your children, your devotion has already been pledged to the idol of busyness. If you're too busy for your brothers and sisters in Christ, your allegiance has been cast with the idol of busyness. If you're too busy to share the message of Jesus with an unbeliever, you're being choked to death by the idol of busyness.

Notice, in contrast, what Paul presented on numerous occasions as the God-envisioned lifestyle of a Christian.

> But we urge you, brothers … to aspire to live quietly, and to mind your own affairs, and to work with your hands, as we instructed you, so that you may live properly before outsiders and be dependent on no one. (1 Thes 4.10–12)

> Now such persons we command and exhort in the Lord Jesus Christ to work in quiet fashion and eat their own bread. (2 Thes 3.12)

> First of all, then, I urge that supplications, prayers, intercessions, and thanksgivings be made for all people, for kings and all who are in high positions, that we may lead a peaceful and quiet life, godly and dignified in every way. (1 Tim 2.1–2)

It's time to be honest. Doesn't "quiet" suggest a manner of life that is the polar opposite to the way most men live in the 21st century? Is there any aspect of your daily routine that could truly be described as *quiet?* Do your best to remember the last time you had any semblance of substantial, uninterrupted "peaceful and quiet" time. How long has it been?

When we stop to calculate the precious little amount of quiet time in our own lives, the peace which is limited too frequently by our own foolish choices, we grow to appreciate why the Savior periodically withdrew to "desolate places" or rose "very early in the morning." It very well may be that such is the only opportunity for truly quiet time.

But is it worth it? The wise man assures us, "Better is a dry morsel with quiet than a house full of feasting and strife" (Prov 17.1). How many people do you know who have more "stuff" than they know what to do with? And how many of those people woke up this morning to miserable home lives? Do you think they would trade the majority of their "stuff" for the blessing of a quiet, peace-filled house? Yeah, me too.

Is It Time for Some Confession?

How is it, then, that we can avoid falling into the "Martha trap" of being "anxious and troubled about many things" which only distract us from the best that God has to offer (Luke 10.41)? How can we dig ourselves out of the materialistic hole of our own making? How can we consistently model for our children a better, more disciplined lifestyle? How can we teach our children and grandchildren to be more responsible with their time and money?

The first step toward banishing the idol of greed from our lives is authentic, heartfelt confession. The initial stride toward placing busyness in its proper perspective is pouring our hearts out to God with the type of humility and transparency modeled by John G. Whittier in his reverent hymn from 1872. Take your time with these beautiful words.

> Dear Lord and Father of mankind,
> Forgive our foolish ways;
> Reclothe us in our rightful mind,
> In purer lives Thy service find,
> In deeper reverence, praise.

In simple trust like theirs who heard
Beside the Syrian sea,
The gracious calling of the Lord,
Let us, like them, without a word,
Rise up and follow Thee.

O Sabbath rest by Galilee,
O calm of hills above,
Where Jesus knelt to share with Thee
The silence of eternity,
Interpreted by love!

Drop Thy still dews of quietness,
Till all our strivings cease;
Take from our souls the strain and stress,
And let our ordered lives confess
The beauty of Thy peace.

Even in 21st century America, ordered lives that have been carefully fashioned in the beauty of God's peace can be a reality. You can be God's man, refined in the fiery disciplines of reverent meditation, humble confession, fervent prayer, and a yielded spirit. You can cling to Jesus as your all-satisfying Treasure. This is life as God envisioned. Are you living that life? If not, why not?

What Would Happen…?

What would happen if an entire generation of Christians force-fully brought their view of money and its purposes back into the framework of God's intentions? John Piper effectively describes our goal as soldiers of the cross and the ever-present obstacles which stand in our way.

Sometimes I use the phrase "wartime lifestyle" or "wartime mind-set." …It tells me that there is a war going on in the world between Christ and Satan, truth and falsehood, belief and un-belief. It tells me that there are weapons to be funded and used, but that these weapons are not swords or guns or bombs but the Gospel and prayer and self-sacrificing love (2 Cor 10.3–5). And it tells me that the stakes of this conflict are higher than any other war in history; they are eternal and infinite: heaven or hell, eternal joy or eternal torment (Matt 25.46).

I need to hear this message again and again, because I drift into a peacetime mind-set as certainly as rain falls down and flames go up. I am wired by nature to love the same toys that the world loves. I start to fit in. I start to love what others love. I start to call earth "home." Before you know it, I am calling luxuries "needs" and using my money just the way unbelievers do. I begin to forget the war. I don't think much about people perishing. Missions and unreached peoples drop out of my mind. I stop dreaming about the triumphs of grace. I sink into a secular mind-set that looks first to what man can do, not what God can do. It is a terrible sickness. And I thank God for those who have forced me again and again toward a wartime mind-set. [1]

Paul was such a man. He told Timothy to instruct disciples of Christ to work in order to provide for their families. "If anyone does not provide for his relatives, and especially for members of his household, he has denied the faith and is worse than an unbeliever" (1 Tim 5.8).

As disciples of Christ, we work to earn money. We earn money to provide for our families. But the divine intention does not rest at that point. Paul's letter to the saints in Ephesus contained further specific instructions. "Let the thief no longer steal, but rather let him labor, doing honest work with his own hands, so that he may have something to share with anyone in need" (Eph 4.28).

As followers of Jesus, we work in honesty to earn money so that we can share with those in need. Has your perspective on the resources of this world been refined to such a degree? What would happen if an entire generation of Christians viewed the money they had to work with in those terms? "We will use what we have to provide for our families and to share with anyone in need. Our aim is to magnify our King through generosity."

What kind of an impact could be had on your marriage if both you and your spouse could grow to view your income in those terms? "We will use what we have to provide for our family and to share with anyone in need. We will not forget that we are at war. We will live above our "save yourself" society. That means less stuff, more hospitality. Less toys, more sharing. Less luxuries, more giving."

How much stress could be lifted if we adopted a more cross-centered view of our resources? How could more discipline lead to more opportunities to serve in the kingdom? What areas of our budgets of time and money could be brought more fully into the pattern of "seeking first the kingdom of God and his righteousness" (Matt 6.33)? The cause of Christ is worthy of a lifetime of spending and being spent for the souls of others (2 Cor 12.15).

In what ways can we more seriously model the Spirit's instruction? "There is great gain in godliness with contentment, for we brought nothing into the world, and we cannot take anything out of the world. But if we have food and clothing, with these we will be content" (1 Tim 6.6–8).

If just one, or two, or three people openly refused to bow down to the idols of covetousness, materialism, and busyness, could it really make that big of a difference?

The Rest of the Story

Hananiah, Mishael and Azariah look each of us in the eye and answer, "Absolutely!" We diverged from their story as they boldly stood before King Nebuchadnezzar and said, "we will not serve your gods or worship the golden image that you have set up" (Dan 3.18). In response, as you can imagine, "Nebuchadnezzar was filled with fury" to the point that "the expression on his face was changed" (Dan 3.19). He ordered the furnace to be heated seven times hotter than normal.

The young men were bound in their cloaks, tunics, hats and other garments and thrown by some of Nebuchadnezzar's mighty men into a burning furnace. Daniel 3.22 tells us that "because the king's order was urgent and the furnace overheated, the flame of the fire killed those men who took up Shadrach, Meshach, and Abednego."

But as the old song suggests, "they wouldn't bow, they wouldn't bend, they wouldn't burn." In astonishment, Nebuchadnezzar said to his counselors, "Did we not cast three men bound into the fire? ...But I see four men unbound, walking in the midst of the fire, and they are not hurt; and the appearance of the fourth is like a son of the gods" (Dan 3.25).

Nebuchadnezzar immediately declared, "Shadrach, Meshach, and Abednego, servants of the Most High God, come out, and come here!" (Dan 3.26). Amazingly, "The hair of their heads was not singed, their cloaks were not harmed, and no smell of fire had come upon them" (Dan 3.27).

Did just three young men who openly refused to bow down to Nebuchadnezzar's idol really make that big of a difference? The answer is found in the pagan king's declaration.

> "Blessed be the God of Shadrach, Meshach, and Abednego, who has sent his angel and delivered his servants, who trusted in him, and set aside the king's command, and yielded up their bodies rather than serve and worship any god except their own God. Therefore I make a decree: Any people, nation, or language that speaks anything against the God of Shadrach, Meshach, and Abednego shall be torn limb from limb, and their houses laid in ruins, for there is no other god who is able to rescue in this way." (Dan 3.28–29)

What would happen if *you* stopped bowing down to the idols of our own culture—covetousness, materialism and busyness? One thing is certain—our King would walk with you, even in the midst of the fire. Beyond that, there's only one way to find out.

8

Jealousy

Playing into the Enemy's Hands by Turning on Each Other

Wrath is fierce and anger is a flood, but who can stand before jealousy? (Prov 27.4, NASB)

What's the natural and logical follow-up to Idolatry 101 in the Boot Camp of integrity? You've found it. Remember one of our keys for survival in the battle for our souls: "Make sure that your character is free from the love of money, being content with what you have" (Heb 13.5, NASB). Easier said than done, right?

As we begin this next phase of our spiritual basic training, to help us dig deep for the root of the problem, we're looked in the eye and asked a simple, sobering question by those who have spent time on the battlefield:

*"How much of the motivation for what you do (or do **not** do) actually stems from what you want other people to think about you?"*

Don't blow that inquiry off. Stop and ask the hard questions. How much of what I say directly stems from what I want other people to think of me? Is my biggest goal to impress others with what comes out of my mouth? To what degree is what I do in God's service actually built on the hope that others will notice and praise me? When it comes to my material possessions, how frequently do I go out and buy something simply because some-body else already has it and I feel left out?

Let me share with you one of the many reasons I appreciate the English Standard Version of the Scriptures. Paul's instructions in Philippians 2.3 are rendered in that translation, "Do nothing from rivalry or conceit, but in humility count others more significant than yourselves."

When I read *rivalry* in that passage for the first time, it hit me right between the eyes. I was used to seeing *selfishness* (NASB) or *selfish ambition* (NKJV). Perhaps it's just me, but *rivalry* struck a stronger cord—a cord that needed to be struck.

Maybe a little bit of background would be helpful. You'd be hard-pressed to find a more competitive person than me, or at least the me of a few years ago. My past is dotted with numerous "battlefield" memories. Playing "war" with my younger brother and a troop of elementary school friends in the backyard. Pitching in little league baseball. Playing guard in the local junior basketball league. Junior high spelling bees. High-school tennis. Basketball several times a week as a teenager. The honor society. The chase for academic esteem among the class of '97. Even episodes from the past month readily come to mind. Video game tournaments. Flag football. Air hockey and ping-pong at a local student center.

Competitiveness seems like it's always been a part of my life and the lives of so many of my closest friends. The older I get, however, the more disgusted I become with the way rivalry affects relationships. Some of us can't seem to differentiate between giving it our all with the ultimate goal of enjoying God-given life and looking to one up, show up or impress whomever happens to be around. Truth be told, most of the bystanders probably couldn't care less.

And yet, how sad when feelings of bitterness over what happened in an inconsequential game yesterday causes awkwardness among brothers in Christ today. Does that even matter? How miserable when someone is constantly looking to impress others with what they can do in a stupid contest. Is that really the point? How tragic when we teach our children by example that their worth is dependent upon how many people they can defeat in any given arena. How do such examples impact the philosophy of success within our sons and daughters? How pitiful when adults consume themselves with what house, car, or latest toy their friends have, and allow such to strain precious relationships. Does anyone really care what kind of car I drive?

We are foolish and shortsighted if we indict only men in the realm of rivalry. How many wives are miserable because their husbands don't make as much as the next woman's husband? How many women are bitter because some acquaintance just moved into a newer, bigger house? How many mothers consume themselves every day with setting up their children in contrast with someone else's children? A word may never be spoken to the object of jealousy and envy, but how much mental energy is wasted on such fruitless comparisons?

Make no mistake about it. The foundational principle of Jealousy 101 is that if integrity has any hope of being born within, selfish ambition, jealousy and rivalry must be forcefully placed before a righteous firing squad. If contentment is the ideal, envy—a feeling of discontent and resentment aroused by a desire for the possessions or qualities of another—is the complete opposite. Just as soldiers of the cross seek to cut envy out of their hearts with the sword of the Spirit, selfish ambition is bred, fertilized and harvested within the hearts of those enslaved by the Adversary. Think of Idolatry 101 and notice the progression:

Seeds of covetousness sprout within because of the jealousy I feel at what a co-worker just bought. I can't stand being around him when he talks about it.

Weeds of materialism begin to spread because my feelings of selfish ambition can't seem to be controlled. I want what he has, regardless of the cost.

I find that a harvest of meaningless busyness is being reaped because my sense of rivalry is driving me to compete with anyone and everyone. I must keep up, no matter the toll.

If we are to survive the war for our souls, we must be forcefully brought to the realization that such is the well-worn path of ridiculous slavery! "Do you not know that if you present yourselves to anyone as obedient slaves, you are slaves of the one whom you obey, either of sin, which leads to death, or of obedience, which leads to righteousness?" (Rom 6.16).

Selfish ambitions are the shackles. Jealousy is the chain. Rivalry is the heavy metal ball on the end. Allow feelings of discontentment and resentment to fester within as you compare your possessions and your qualities with another and you'll find yourself "sold under sin" (Rom 7.14). One day, you'll wake up and find yourself heavily entrenched behind Enemy lines.

Long before Shakespeare referred to envy as "the green sickness," the Preacher shared his conclusions on the emptiness of such uncontrolled emotions. "Then I saw that all toil and all skill in work comes from a man's envy of his neighbor. This also is vanity and a striving after wind" (Ecc 4.4).

Times haven't changed, have they? Jealousy is still the path to misery and emptiness. Never-ending efforts to win each contest of meaningless rivalry are likened to chasing the wind wherever it blows. Do you want to be miserable for the rest of your life? Base your happiness and contentment on a competition with the possessions, qualities, and accomplishments of others. Just recognize that "even now you are not yet ready, for you are still of the flesh. For while there is jealousy and strife among you, are you not of the flesh and behaving only in a human way?" (1 Cor 3.3).

You're not the first. That fruitless struggle is nearly as old as the world. The sad stories of defeat and betrayal abound. And here's the point. The wise soldier of character will take the time to learn from the mistakes of history lest he repeat them to his own destruction.

Jealous of Someone Else's Service

Now Abel was a keeper of sheep, and Cain a worker of the ground. In the course of time Cain brought to the LORD an offering of the fruit of the ground, and Abel also brought of the firstborn of his flock and of their fat portions. And the LORD had regard for Abel and his offering, but for Cain and his offering he had no regard (Gen 4.2–5).

Do you remember the subtitle of this chapter? *Playing into the Enemy's Hands by Turning on Each Other.* How tragic that just three chapters into the Biblical narrative we find that tragic scenario played out right before our eyes.

Two brothers. The first human offspring in the history of the world. Both are willing to work. Both bring a sacrifice of the fruits of their labor to the Creator. Younger brother Abel's offering is accepted. Older brother Cain's is not. "So Cain became very angry, and his countenance fell" (Gen 4.5, NASB).

It's not hard to imagine what could have been going through Cain's mind. "What? I worked hard too! Why should he be accepted and not me; after all, I'm the oldest. What does he have that I don't? What can I do now to reestablish myself as superior to him? He may have won this round, but I'll get even!"

It's also not hard to spot the fundamental problem in this scenario, is it? The flaw in our own aim lives on. Rather than focusing on God's expectations, we naturally sharpen our eyes squarely on ourselves in relation to others. We convince ourselves that this—the rivalry between human beings—is the real battle. This is where true success can be found. If I can just find a way to one-up my opponent, I'll feel better about myself.

Those are lies. They spawn from the "father of lies" (John 8.44) who first revealed himself in Genesis 3. The effect of believing the lies? Brother turns against brother.

As the drama unfolds, the Creator himself makes an attempt to recenter Cain on the only thing that really matters. "Why are you angry, and why has your face fallen? If you do well, will you not be accepted? And if you do not do well, sin is crouching at the door. Its desire is for you, but you must rule over it" (Gen 4.6–7).

God's reasoning isn't difficult to understand, is it? "It's not about Abel, Cain. It's not about competition. It's about you and your relationship with me. It's about your choice to do what's right and trusting in me to accept you for it. If you do what you know to be right, all will work itself out. Stop worrying about everyone else and worry about ruling your own emotions and actions."

Such was obviously good advice that should have been heeded, but you already know how the story ends. "Cain spoke to Abel his brother. And when they were in the field, Cain rose up against his brother Abel and killed him" (Gen 4.8).

Let's bring the focus back to our own Boot Camp for a moment. Even the most senseless military confrontations of the past can teach powerful lessons for the future. That's why soldiers study the ins and outs of previous victories and defeats. The same is true with this monumental failure. Modern men of integrity will take the time to learn from the tragedy. How foolish to be jealous of someone else when they're simply doing what's right! How easily our envy can get the best of us. God expects us to quit worrying about where we stand in relation to the next guy and get our own selves straightened out. Sin is just around the corner. Its intent is to inflict destruction, but we can conquer! We can control ourselves by not allowing our anger and disappointment to be directed at others. It's not about them, it's about each one's personal relationship with God.

How sadly ironic when a soldier of the Lord turns on his brother in jealousy over what is being accomplished in the service of the kingdom! The biggest turncoats may actually be preachers of the gospel who seem to thrive on a sense of rivalry among themselves. Two thousand years ago, Paul spoke of those who "preach Christ from envy and rivalry... not sincerely, but thinking to afflict me in my imprisonment" (Phil 1.15–17). The spirit of rivalry among preachers, both young and old, is alive and well. What bigger adventure could there be in missing the point?

The pawns in this game of senseless comparisons? The size of congregations, the ornateness of the church buildings, the reputation of the preachers, educational backgrounds, salaries, houses, and even the growth and progress which is accomplished through diligent labor in the gospel. Many disciples of Christ seem to model themselves to a much greater degree after prima donna sports athletes than Jesus Christ.

If we are to have any success in pressing the battle lines of the kingdom forward, we must learn to operate from a singular focus: it's not about me! It's certainly not about how I stack up in comparison with others. It's not about the congregation with which I labor. It's not about a building. It's not about personal accomplishments. It's not about competition. Paul's words in 1 Corinthians 3.1–7 seem eerily appropriate still.

> But I, brothers, could not address you as spiritual people, but as people of the flesh, as infants in Christ. I fed you with milk, not solid food, for you were not ready for it. And even now you are not yet ready, for you are still of the flesh. For while there is jealousy and strife among you, are you not of the flesh and behaving only in a human way? For when one says, "I follow Paul," and another, "I follow Apollos," are you not being merely human?
>
> What then is Apollos? What is Paul? Servants through whom you believed, as the Lord assigned to each. I planted, Apollos watered, but God gave the growth. So neither he who plants nor he who waters is anything, but only God who gives the growth.

Every soldier of the cross must remember, this is about God. This is about his kingdom. This is about learning to work together. This is about being mature enough to "rejoice with those who rejoice" and "weep with those who weep" (Rom 12.15). This is about remembering who the real Enemy is.

Jealous of Someone Else's Blessings

Are you beginning to see how the point of this chapter naturally builds on the message of the last? Someone is always going to have more than you—a bigger house, a faster car, a fatter wallet, a wider TV. Someone is always going to be more than you—smarter, thinner, more athletic, better looking, more privileged. Someone is always going to be treated more preferentially than you feel you've been treated—at work, in society, perhaps even in your own family.

We may not always understand why, but we can be confident in this fact—if we allow possessions, accomplishments, and privileges to gain the status of idolatry in our lives, our natural reaction when we see those items and qualities in others will be envy and jealousy. The psalmist readily confessed this tendency in his own life:

> For I was envious of the arrogant
>> when I saw the prosperity of the wicked.
>
> For they have no pangs until death;
>> their bodies are fat and sleek.
>
> They are not in trouble as others are;
>> they are not stricken like the rest of mankind…
>
> Behold, these are the wicked;
>> always at ease, they increase in riches. (Psa 73.3–5, 12)

Do the math. The formula is really quite simple:

I live for possessions, worldly accomplishments, and the praise of men

+

My happiness depends on how I stack up to other people in those areas

=

I can't figure out why I'm always jealous and envious of other people.

In Sexual Immorality 101, Joseph was our instructor. You'll recall that we found him in Egypt being tempted by Potiphar's wife. But if you know your Old Testament, you'll recall that Joseph wasn't native to Egypt—his homeland was Canaan. So how did he wind up hundreds of miles away from home in the first place?

We haven't even gotten out of Genesis before encountering this second destructive scene of jealousy between brothers. At seventeen years old, Joseph was without question the favorite son of his father Israel. He was "the son of his old age" and the offspring of Israel's preferred wife, Rachel. "Israel loved Joseph more than any other of his sons," and the parental favoritism was manifested in the gift of a "robe of many colors" (Gen 37.3). Of course, Joseph's brothers noticed. "When his brothers saw that their father loved him more than all his brothers, they hated him and could not speak peacefully to him" (Gen 37.4).

The seeds of bitter jealousy and resentment continued to quietly grow on this unsteady family foundation:

Now Joseph had a dream, and when he told it to his brothers they hated him even more. He said to them, "Hear this dream that I have dreamed: Behold, we were binding sheaves in the field, and behold, my sheaf arose and stood upright. And behold, your sheaves gathered around it and bowed down to my sheaf." His brothers said to him, "Are you indeed to reign over us? Or are you indeed to rule over us?" So they hated him even more for his dreams and for his words.

Then he dreamed another dream and told it to his brothers and said, "Behold, I have dreamed another dream. Behold, the sun, the moon, and eleven stars were bowing down to me." But when he told it to his father and to his brothers, his father rebuked him and said to him, "What is this dream that you have dreamed? Shall I and your mother and your brothers indeed come to bow ourselves to the ground before you?" And his brothers were jealous of him. (Gen 37.5–11)

Comparisons of themselves to Joseph and his privileges led to jealousy. Jealousy led to hatred. Hatred led to a plot. The plot was to end in murder. Sound familiar?

They saw him from afar, and before he came near to them they conspired against him to kill him. They said to one another, "Here comes this dreamer. Come now, let us kill him and throw him into one of the pits. Then we will say that a fierce animal has devoured him, and we will see what will become of his dreams." But when Reuben heard it, he rescued him out of their hands, saying, "Let us not take his life." And Reuben said to them, "Shed no blood; throw him into this pit here in the wilderness, but do not lay a hand on him"—that he might rescue him out of their hand to restore him to his father. So when Joseph came to his brothers, they stripped him of his robe, the robe of many colors that he wore. And they took him and threw him into a pit. The pit was empty; there was no water in it.

Then they sat down to eat. And looking up they saw a caravan of Ishmaelites coming from Gilead. …Then Judah said to his brothers, "What profit is it if we kill our brother and conceal his blood? Come, let us sell him to the Ishmaelites, and let not our hand be upon him, for he is our brother, our own flesh." And his brothers listened to him. Then Midianite traders passed by. And they drew Joseph up and lifted him out of the pit, and sold him to the Ishmaelites for twenty shekels of silver. They took Joseph to Egypt. (Gen 37.18–28)

Sold as a slave. Carried against his will to Egypt. Separated from his father. Distanced from everything he had ever known. Faced with great temptations to sin. Years spent in prison. A life forever altered. All spawned from a consuming sense of jealousy and rivalry between brothers.

Don't write off that tragic account as nothing more than ancient history. Now you are in the midst of the struggle. Be humble enough to learn from the mistakes of others before you take another step on the battlefield for your soul. "Wrath is fierce and anger is a flood, but who can stand before jealousy?" (Prov 27.4, NASB). James is one veteran who seeks to prep us for the war ahead:

> But if you have bitter jealousy and selfish ambition in your heart, do not be arrogant and so lie against the truth. This wisdom is not that which comes down from above, but is earthly, natural, demonic. For where jealousy and selfish ambition exist, there is disorder and every evil thing. (James 3.14–16, NASB)

Enough people have suffered at the hands of the Enemy because they could not handle their intense envy over the blessings of someone else. Disorder and every vile practice have been the result. The history of past defeats can be plainly studied. Will you learn from them before it's too late?

Jealous of Someone Else's Reputation

You're familiar with David's great victory over Goliath, the Philistine giant (1 Sam 17). While we may frequently spend time mining that wonderful story of courage for practical lessons and then quickly move on to another Biblical account in search of further examples, the narrative continues, and it gets ugly.

As they were coming home, when David returned from striking down the Philistine, the women came out of all the cities of Israel, singing and dancing, to meet King Saul, with tambourines, with songs of joy, and with musical instruments. And the women sang to one another as they celebrated,

"Saul has struck down his thousands,
  and David his ten thousands."

And Saul was very angry, and this saying displeased him. He said, "They have ascribed to David ten thousands, and to me they have ascribed thousands, and what more can he have but the kingdom?" And Saul eyed David from that day on. (1 Sam 18.6–9)

Here it is. The first root of so many wicked actions in which we find Saul engaged for the rest of his life—fruitless comparisons of himself with young David, nagging feelings of inferiority, bitter jealousy, jaded inner dialogue which began to fester beneath the surface, constant strong suspicions that grew only stronger.

It wasn't long before the destructive mix began to overflow.

The next day a harmful spirit from God rushed upon Saul, and he raved within his house while David was playing the lyre, as he did day by day. Saul had his spear in his hand. And Saul hurled the spear, for he thought, "I will pin David to the wall." But David evaded him twice. (1 Sam 18.10–11)

Already we see a man out of control, and the more he compares himself with David, the more he fears him. The more he fears the young man, the more desperate he feels. The more desperate he feels, the stronger his actions become. He sends David to battle against the Philistines, hoping that he will eventually be killed (1 Sam 18.17). He uses two of his own daughters as "a snare" against David (1 Sam 18.17–25). He throws a spear at him on a third occasion (1 Sam 19.8–10). He sets a watch over David's house with instructions to kill him the next morning (1 Sam 19.11–17). He becomes intensely angry with his own son, Jonathan, when it's made clear that he is helping to keep David safe, eventually throwing a spear at him as well (1 Sam 20.30–34). He commands that eighty-five priests be killed on the suspicion that they are sympathetic to David, along with their city—men and women, children and infants (1 Sam 22.6–19). He becomes so desperate that he disguises himself and consults a medium—one of the very deviants he had worked to expel from the land—as to what he should do next (1 Sam 28). Finally, he is badly wounded by Philistine archers, and rather than being captured and tortured by the enemy, he determines to end his life by falling on his own sword (1 Sam 31). What a tragic example of a man driven uncontrollably by comparisons!

In contrast, look closer at Jonathan, a young man whose soul "was knit to the soul of David, and Jonathan loved him as his own soul" (1 Sam 18.1). Imagine the dilemma this young man faced. His loyalty was severely tested. His bond with David, severely challenged. His father, the King, was consumed with jealousy, completely disrespecting and even trying to kill his best friend.

> And Jonathan told David, "Saul my father seeks to kill you. Therefore be on your guard in the morning. Stay in a secret place and hide yourself. And I will go out and stand beside my father in the field where you are, and I will speak to my father about you. And if I learn anything I will tell you." (1 Sam 19.2–3)

Despite the influence of his own flesh and blood, Jonathan was a man of integrity, a man who wanted only to do the right thing. It's one thing to say that, but remember what was at stake. Jonathan was heir to the throne!

> Saul's anger was kindled against Jonathan, and he said to him, "You son of a perverse, rebellious woman, do I not know that you have chosen the son of Jesse to your own shame, and to the shame of your mother's nakedness? For as long as the son of Jesse lives on the earth, neither you nor your kingdom shall be established. Therefore send and bring him to me, for he shall surely die." Then Jonathan answered Saul his father, "Why should he be put to death? What has he done?" (1 Sam 20.30–32)

Despite the reasonings of his father, Jonathan, as a man of integrity, realized that David was not deserving of death. David was suffering wrongfully at the hands of his father. Jonathan's character and loyalty prompted him to unashamedly stand up for his friend. And when he did, "Saul hurled his spear at him to strike him. So Jonathan knew that his father was determined to put David to death" (1 Sam 20.33).

Jonathan understood. He knew the politics of the situation. He was aware of David's enormous popularity with the people. He could easily recognize that as long as David was alive, his own ascendancy to the throne of Israel was threatened.

But Jonathan was content in that fact. So much more than a political rival, David was a dear friend. Even if it meant taking a back seat to the son of Jesse, Jonathan would not allow the jealousy he had seen so powerfully modeled in his father or his own selfish ambitions to destroy his friendship: "Jonathan, Saul's son, rose and went to David at Horesh, and strengthened his hand in God. And he said to him, 'Do not fear, for the hand of Saul my father shall not find you. You shall be king over Israel, and I shall be next to you'" (1 Sam 23.16–17).

What a powerful example of selfless integrity! What character Jonathan possessed! His love for his friend was greater than his love for prestige. His care for David was greater than any desire to take the throne of Israel through wicked means.

Jealous of Someone Else's Restoration

As beautiful as Jonathan's example is, one of the saddest Biblical depictions of jealousy we can find is provided in Jesus' series of "lost" parables (Luke 15). You're familiar with the story. A man has two sons. The younger requests that his father give him his inheritance at once, as if his father had already passed away. He takes his portion of the father's assets, journeys to a far country and squanders his property in reckless, lustful living.

Eventually, a terrible famine hits the countryside, but the young man has spent everything he has. In a desperate effort to survive, he contracts himself out to feed someone else's pigs—unclean animals to the Jews. He longs to be fed even with the slop of the pigs, but no one will give him anything.

The turning point of the story is, of course, how the prodigal comes to himself. He clearly remembers how his father had hired servants with more than enough to eat, and here he is, perishing with hunger! He determines that he will go back to his father, confess his foolishness and request to be made as one of those servants.

While he is still a long way off, his father sees him and is overcome with compassion. He runs to his son, embraces him and kisses him. In spite of his son's request, the father commands that the best robe be brought. Bring a ring for his hand and shoes for his feet! Prepare the fattened calf for a feast! The time has come for a celebration! The emotion behind the father's declaration is evident: "'For this my son was dead, and is alive again; he was lost, and is found.' And they began to celebrate" (Luke 15.11–24).

However, the story has a dark twist at the end.

> Now his older son was in the field, and as he came and drew near to the house, he heard music and dancing. And he called one of the servants and asked what these things meant. And he said to him, "Your brother has come, and your father has killed the fattened calf, because he has received him back safe and sound." But he was angry and refused to go in. His father came out and entreated him, but he answered his father, "Look, these many years I have served you, and I never disobeyed your command, yet you never gave me a young goat, that I might celebrate with my friends. But when this son of yours came, who has devoured your property with prostitutes, you killed the fattened calf for him!" (Luke 15.25–30)

Do you remember the definition of *envy*? "A feeling of discontent and resentment aroused by a desire for the possessions or qualities of another." The young man's own brother has returned home, but he refuses to take any part in the celebration. And what's the source of his misery? Comparisons. "These many years I have served you. I never disobeyed your command. Just look at what this son of yours has done with his blessings. Now you have the audacity to celebrate his return? You never threw a party like this for me!" Such are the reasonings of a spiritual baby, but such babies are born in every generation.

> For right now, friends, I'm completely frustrated by your unspiritual dealings with each other and with God. You're acting like infants in relation to Christ, capable of nothing much more than nursing at the breast. Well, then, I'll nurse you since you don't seem capable of anything more. As long as you grab for what makes you feel good or makes you look important, are you really much different than a babe at the breast, content only when everything's going your way? ...Aren't you being totally infantile? (1 Cor 3.1–3, MSG)

The older brother of the prodigal was being totally infantile. Lost in the foolish shortsightedness of his envious perspective was the fact that his own younger brother had come home seeking redemption. The one who might as well have been dead was alive again! He who seemed to be hopelessly lost had now been found! But the older brother couldn't see it, couldn't open his heart wide enough to appreciate his younger brother's humility and his father's grace. His affections had been choked by the thorns of jealousy and resentment.

Why did Jesus tell the story in the first place? "Now the tax collectors and sinners were all drawing near to hear him. And the Pharisees and the scribes grumbled, saying, 'This man receives sinners and eats with them'" (Luke 15.1–2). How dare the One who would claim to be Israel's Messiah spurn the company of the elite for the lowly! What was one of the very roots of the Pharisees' hatred of Jesus? Even Pilate "knew that it was out of envy that they had delivered him up" (Matt 27.18).

The point? Learn the lessons of the past before you fall prey as well. How disgusting to our Father when his children look down on those who are willing to receive the message of the gospel. How pitiful our motivation when we find ourselves in competition with those determined to share the "good news." How dismal the future of the man who dies in such a state!

The Prescription for "The Green Sickness"

In the midst of it all, Paul gives a simple prescription: "Do nothing from rivalry or conceit, but in humility count others more significant than yourselves. Let each of you look not only to his own interests, but also to the interests of others" (Phil 2.3–4).

And so, the question stands:

*"How much of the motivation for what you do (or do **not** do) actually stems from what you want other people to think about you?"*

What would happen if we could learn to stop comparing ourselves with the people around us and actually count them as more significant than ourselves?

I appreciate the New Living Translation's paraphrase of Paul's words: "Don't be selfish; don't live to make a good impression on others. Be humble, thinking of others as better than yourself. Don't think only about your own affairs, but be interested in others, too, and what they are doing."

I've been blessed with a wife who has graciously and patiently helped me to see what a fool I've made of myself when I operate in the spirit of stupid rivalry. I've been blessed with friends who still claim me as a friend, even though I acted like an idiot during a meaningless game. I hope you have someone like that in your life. Let's pray for fellow soldiers who are bold enough to point out the green sickness in us when they see it.

Open your eyes. The people who are "living to make a good impression on others" are all around us. Our King assures us that they "have received their reward" (Matt 6.2, 5, 16). Recognize how exceedingly ugly and destructive the spirit of rivalry can be. But just as intently as you look at others, honestly look in the mirror. Who are *you* trying to impress?

9

Anger

When the Going Gets Tough, Can I Control My Emotions?

Whoever is slow to anger is better than the mighty, and he who rules his spirit than he who takes a city (Prov 16.32).

Ask any soldier to list the fundamental lessons of Boot Camp and you're sure to hear at least something about learning to control your emotions. Warriors in training are pushed to the limit by their allies because unwavering discipline will be sorely needed on the battlefields of the future. The reality of war is that horrors beyond description could be waiting just over the next hill, and when a solider comes face to face with a bitter struggle to the death, he cannot be governed by raw emotion. The veteran who lives to fight another day has learned to objectively control his feelings, even when the going is at its toughest.

The same is true in spiritual warfare. History tells stories of even the occasional fool who was able to take a city. But the one who is truly "slow to anger," the man "who rules his spirit," that is a man walking in the pathway of integrity.

"Whoever is slow to anger has great understanding, but he who has a hasty temper exalts folly" (Prov 14.29). You don't need to read that wise statement in Scripture to know that it's true. The man with a hasty temper is bound to make mistakes and end up looking like a fool. We've all seen it. More specifically, we've all played the role. That's precisely why our own Boot Camp experience wouldn't be complete without carefully studying a critical confrontation from the Old Testament that nearly ended in bloodshed because the going got tough, and emotions began to run wild.

The Setting

"Now Samuel died." Those are the jarring words at the opening of 1 Samuel 25. Place yourself in young David's shoes. His stabilizing mentor is gone. Saul continues to hunt him each day like a wild animal. In his own words, "There is but a step between me and death" (1 Sam 20.3), and a great stronghold of spiritual encouragement has been irreplaceably taken out of David's life.

Perhaps you know the feeling all too well. Vital crutches upon which you've depended in the past are forcibly removed from your life. Feelings of despair, confusion and hopelessness cloud the horizon of your spirit. Add to the equation the fact that David couldn't publicly assemble and mourn for Samuel like the rest of Israel at the risk of his own life, and it's not hard to imagine his state of mind. David is a man strung out and on edge.

> Then David rose and went down to the wilderness of Paran. And there was a man in Maon whose business was in Carmel. The man was very rich; he had three thousand sheep and a thousand goats. He was shearing his sheep in Carmel. Now the name of the man was Nabal, and the name of his wife Abigail. The woman was discerning and beautiful, but the man was harsh and badly behaved. (1 Sam 25.1–3)

Nabal is a "harsh" man. Just listen to the way that word is translated in other Old Testament passages: cruel, difficult, fierce, hard, obstinate, severe, stubborn. That's Nabal. He's very rich, but badly behaved. He lays claim to 3,000 sheep and 1,000 goats, but his own name gives a strikingly accurate description of his character. *Nabal* means "fool." More than one time in 1 Samuel 25 he is referred to as "worthless."

Nabal's wife, on the other hand, is not only outwardly beautiful, but "discerning." Behind the pretty face is a perceptive mind. She's known for her good judgment and wisdom. When the going gets tough, she possesses precisely what is needed in the midst of conflict—control over her own emotions.

David's Request

David heard in the wilderness that Nabal was shearing his sheep. So David sent ten young men. And David said to the young men, "Go up to Carmel, and go to Nabal and greet him in my name. And thus you shall greet him: 'Peace be to you, and peace be to your house, and peace be to all that you have. I hear that you have shearers. Now your shepherds have been with us, and we did them no harm, and they missed nothing all the time they were in Carmel. Ask your young men, and they will tell you. Therefore let my young men find favor in your eyes, for we come on a feast day. Please give whatever you have at hand to your servants and to your son David.'" (1 Sam 25.4–8)

Remember the context. In the eyes of the highest authority in the land, David and his men are rogues. Traitors to the crown. Outlaws who are constantly on the run. It's no mistake that David takes great care with his opening words. "Peace" is spoken three times in his first statement to Nabal.

David makes it known that his men had voluntarily protected Nabal's flocks from any wild animals or raiders while in the area. Nabal's own servants could readily testify to their treatment from David and his men. Now, the time to shear the sheep has come. The flocks will be counted and rewards handed down by the master to the shepherds. David's humble request is that support also be extended to his men for the protection they've provided.

Remember, David and his men have been forced to live in the wilderness for their own protection. They would be in constant need of the most basic necessities of life, and here is an opportunity for some give-and-take to meet those needs. David even ends his plea by referring to himself as a son and his men as servants. Good start to the dialogue, right?

Emotions Quickly Spin Out Of Control

And Nabal answered David's servants, "Who is David? Who is the son of Jesse? There are many servants these days who are breaking away from their masters. Shall I take my bread and my water and my meat that I have killed for my shearers and give it to men who come from I do not know where?" (1 Sam 25.10–11)

Nabal not only denies David's request, but laces his denial with personal insults: "Who is David?" It's evident that Nabal knew exactly who David was by his mention of David's father, Jesse. But in Nabal's eyes, David is a traitor to the crown, a runaway slave from his rightful master, a renegade deserter from Saul's army. Why should Nabal share his bread and his water and his meat intended for his shearers with a bunch of AWOL rogues in the wilderness?

So David's young men turned away and came back and told him all this. And David said to his men, "Every man strap on his sword!" And every man of them strapped on his sword. David also strapped on his sword. And about four hundred men went up after David, while two hundred remained with the baggage. (1 Sam 25.13)

Irritated. That's what David is. Irritated and angry. "Who is David? I'll show him who David is! We'll see how he likes it when 400 guerilla soldiers show up on his doorstep."

You know the feeling, don't you? You've extended an act of kindness to someone who essentially spits in the face of your courtesy, and it bothers you. The more you think about it, the more bothered you become. The more bothered you become, the more your anger and resentment grow. And then, the opportunity arises to lash out. To get even. To clearly show just how mad you really are.

That's David at this point. He's had his fill of dealing with vengeful, unfair men and he's going to teach Nabal a lesson the hard way. After refusing to retaliate for months, even as King Saul had done everything in his power to kill him, David has finally lost his patience. He's ready to explode, and Nabal appears to be the perfect target.

> Now David had said, "Surely in vain have I guarded all that this fellow has in the wilderness, so that nothing was missed of all that belonged to him, and he has returned me evil for good. God do so to the enemies of David and more also, if by morning I leave so much as one male of all who belong to him." (1 Sam 25.21–22)

The going has gotten tough and one of the great heroes of the Old Testament has lost his cool. The soldier after God's own heart who usually inquired of Jehovah before going into battle has allowed his temper to flare and overrule the way he knows he should act. There's one thing, and only one thing on his mind—revenge. And if it's up to David in his present state of mind, his revenge will end in mass bloodshed.

"Whoever Is Slow To Anger Is Better Than The Mighty"

But one of the young men told Abigail, Nabal's wife, "Behold, David sent messengers out of the wilderness to greet our master, and he railed at them. Yet the men were very good to us, and we suffered no harm, and we did not miss anything when we were in the fields, as long as we went with them. They were a wall to us both by night and by day, all the while we were with them keeping the sheep. Now therefore know this and consider what you should do, for harm is determined against our master and against all his house, and he is such a worthless man that one cannot speak to him." (1 Sam 25.14–17)

Talk about a contrast! Nabal hears David's request and sneers at him with insults. David hears Nabal's insults and is immediately prepared to strike back with violence. But Abigail is known to be a logical woman who will "consider" what should be done before she acts. Nabal is such a worthless man, he won't listen to anybody. David is riding in a rage towards Nabal with sword already in hand. But Abigail will use wisdom and kindness to unravel the crisis.

> Then Abigail made haste and took two hundred loaves and two skins of wine and five sheep already prepared and five seahs of parched grain and a hundred clusters of raisins and two hundred cakes of figs, and laid them on donkeys. And she said to her young men, "Go on before me; behold, I come after you." (1 Sam 25.18–19)

What an impressive woman! In our own age of pizza deliveries to the house and 24-hour fast food from a drive-through, Abigail continues to stand out as an excellent and virtuous provider for others. Would she have had help? Undoubtedly! But her command of the moment and willingness to act is what sets her apart. She knows the situation demands speed and doesn't even want the servants to wait for her. "But she did not tell her husband Nabal" (1 Sam 25.19).

The husband of an excellent woman has no greater source of help or insight than his wife: "She does him good, and not harm, all the days of her life. …Strength and dignity are her clothing, and she laughs at the time to come. She opens her mouth with wisdom, and the teaching of kindness is on her tongue" (Prov 31.12, 25–26).

The excellent wife has her husband's best interest always at heart. At times, in order to help him become more fully the man God intends, she must help him see unpleasant things about himself. In select circumstances, the wisest thing she can do is work on his behalf without even saying a word—especially when he's too selfish and ignorant to listen. In doing just that, Abigail literally saves the life of her husband.

> And as she rode on the donkey and came down under cover of the mountain, behold, David and his men came down toward her, and she met them. …When Abigail saw David, she hurried and got down from the donkey and fell before David on her face and bowed to the ground. She fell at his feet and said, "On me alone, my lord, be the guilt. Please let your servant speak in your ears, and hear the words of your servant. Let not my lord regard this worthless fellow, Nabal, for as his name is, so is he. Nabal is his name, and folly is with him." (1 Sam 25.20, 23–25)

Abigail wisely takes the initiative when she first sees David. Without waiting to see if an attack will come, she immediately gets off of her donkey and falls on her face to the ground. She pleads that the responsibility for Nabal's shameful slight be placed on her even though she had nothing to do with it. Significantly, Abigail is also readily willing to admit the faults of her husband.

We can all see the faults in other people and their families, but the humble and wise servant of God is willing to acknowledge the weaknesses in his or her own life and family. What good is accomplished by a wife who refuses to acknowledge the faults of her husband? Is good and not harm done when we overlook the chinks in our armor that need immediate attention and repair? Humility, intelligence, tact, sacrifice—these are the tools Abigail uses to diffuse this crisis. Just listen to her speech:

> "But I your servant did not see the young men of my lord, whom you sent. Now then, my lord, as the LORD lives, and as your soul lives, because the LORD has restrained you from bloodguilt and from saving with your own hand, now then let your enemies and those who seek to do evil to my lord be as Nabal. And now let this present that your servant has brought to my lord be given to the young men who follow my lord. Please forgive the trespass of your servant. For the LORD will certainly make my lord a sure house, because my lord is fighting the battles of the LORD, and evil shall not be found in you so long as you live. If men rise up to pursue you and to seek your life, the life of my lord shall be bound in the bundle of the living in the care of the LORD your God. And the lives of your enemies he shall sling out as from the hollow of a sling. And when the LORD has done to my lord according to all the good that he has spoken concerning you and has appointed you prince over Israel, my lord shall have no cause of grief or pangs of conscience for having shed blood without cause or for my lord taking vengeance himself. And when the LORD has dealt well with my lord, then remember your servant." (1 Sam 25.25–31)

Abigail's plea to David is a living example of several of the wise statements contained in Proverbs 25:

A word fitly spoken is like apples of gold in a setting of silver. Like a gold ring or an ornament of gold is a wise reprover to a listening ear. (vv 11–12)

With patience a ruler may be persuaded, and a soft tongue will break a bone. (v 15)

If your enemy is hungry, give him bread to eat, and if he is thirsty, give him water to drink, for you will heap burning coals on his head, and the LORD will reward you. (vv 21–22)

The wisdom behind those proverbs is even shown in David's reaction to Abigail's speech:

"Blessed be the LORD, the God of Israel, who sent you this day to meet me! Blessed be your discretion, and blessed be you, who have kept me this day from bloodguilt and from avenging myself with my own hand! …Go up in peace to your house. See, I have obeyed your voice, and I have granted your petition." (1 Sam 25.32–35)

As we bring the focus back to our own Boot Camp experience, what can we learn from studying this ancient conflict that nearly ended in vengeful bloodshed?

You Won't Always Be Treated the Way You Feel You Deserve

Isn't that why David got upset in the first place? It's not hard to guess how his mind could have raced as he charged towards Nabal with the intent to kill. "Just look at what we've done for this worthless ingrate! He doesn't even realize how easily we could have stolen everything he had in the wilderness. What did I ever do to him? Doesn't he know who I am? It's time someone brought this fool down a notch!"

Men who would travel the pathway of integrity must learn to live with this reality of spiritual warfare—you won't always be treated in the way you feel you deserve. People will be rude with their mouths. Your deeds of kindness will sometimes go unnoticed at best, scorned at worst. You may be lied about. You might be intentionally misrepresented. You could be the subject of rumors that spread far beyond the scope of your imagination. You will be underappreciated. You will be overworked. But, "Good sense makes one slow to anger, and it is his glory to overlook an offense" (Prov 19.11).

It was David himself who would write in the latter part of his life, "Refrain from anger, and forsake wrath! Fret not yourself; it tends only to evil" (Psa 37.8). It was the righteous Branch of David's bloodline who challenged an audience in Galilee:

> "Blessed are those who are persecuted for righteousness' sake, for theirs is the kingdom of heaven. Blessed are you when others revile you and persecute you and utter all kinds of evil against you falsely on my account. Rejoice and be glad, for your reward is great in heaven, for so they persecuted the prophets who were before you." (Matt 5.10–12)

Do you want to wage the war for your soul with honor and dignity? If so, you must realize that you will never be treated in every circumstance, by every person, the way you feel you deserve. It's in the Training Manual. It's no mystery. It will happen. All you can worry about is yourself and your own conduct. Your mission is straightforward and clear-cut. "Whatever you wish that others would do to you, do also to them, for this is the Law and the Prophets" (Matt 7.12). Our King has been there. "When they hurled their insults at him, he did not retaliate; when he suffered, he made no threats. Instead, he entrusted himself to him who judges justly" (1 Pet 2.23, NIV). The same divine expectation rests upon our shoulders.

Men of Integrity Think Before They Act

Isn't that what Abigail encouraged David to do? "Think of what you could be throwing away, David! The Lord is already working to make a strong house for you. He cares about you! He will continue to be with you and fight for you. But it can all be thrown away right here on the slopes of Carmel! Is it worth the grief you'll feel? Will the pangs of conscience to come be worth what you gain? You're about to shed blood without cause! Is it your place to take your own vengeance?"

Of course, David knew the answers to those questions, just as you and I know what we ought to do in such circumstances. We know how destructive unfiltered wrath can be. We're painfully aware of our own foolish faults. We've seen the harm that bitter retaliation can inflict. But at times, there's a sad disparity between what we know to be right and what we're willing to do in the moment.

David had said just one chapter earlier to Saul, "May the Lord judge between me and you, may the Lord avenge me against you, but my hand shall not be against you" (1 Sam 24.12). As a man after God's own heart, David knew the path he should take. But like so many of us, he started to act before he thought. On that day, in that situation, after hearing those words, he was pushed over the edge. He was content to react and sort out the pieces afterwards. The man after God's own heart was willing to take his affairs out of God's hands and avenge himself with his own.

Here's where the rubber meets the road. The pathways of integrity don't afford such a luxury. "Be not quick in your spirit to become angry, for anger lodges in the bosom of fools" (Ecc 7.9). Wisdom calls the one who ignores such advice hot-tempered: "A hot-tempered man stirs up strife, but he who is slow to anger quiets contention" (Prov 15.18). It doesn't take much to stir up the attitude and emotions of a hot-tempered man. It was Aristotle who said 300 years before Jesus walked the earth, "Anyone can become angry. That is easy. But to be angry with the right person, to the right degree, at the right time, for the right purpose and in the right way—that is not easy."

The rules of engagement in the Lord's army have been clearly defined by James, a veteran of the struggle. "Know this, my beloved brothers: let every person be quick to hear, slow to speak, slow to anger; for the anger of man does not produce the righteousness that God requires" (Jas 1.19–20).

The point is profound in its simplicity. Think before you act! Seek to understand before you speak. Listen—*really* listen—to what is being said instead of simply formulating your next comeback. Any fool can act out of anger. That's the pathway of the natural man, but your Creator is holding you to a higher standard.

The apostle Paul masterfully described the constant struggle between our fleshly impulses and our knowledge of God's expectations.

> I say, walk by the Spirit, and you will not gratify the desires of the flesh. For the desires of the flesh are against the Spirit, and the desires of the Spirit are against the flesh, for these are opposed to each other, to keep you from doing the things you want to do. (Gal 5.16–17)

Our flesh is perfectly content in dwelling upon our mistreatment at the hands of others. The Spirit leads us along the pathway of forbearance. Our flesh welcomes and waters the seeds of bitterness and resentment. The Spirit beckons us to walk in the footsteps of kindness and compassion. Our flesh thrills at the thought of retaliation or even one-upping our antagonist. The Spirit invites us to forgive and move on.

Read these words of James with Nabal, Abigail and David in mind:

> Who is wise and understanding among you? By his good conduct let him show his works in the meekness of wisdom. But if you have bitter jealousy and selfish ambition in your hearts, do not boast and be false to the truth. This is not the wisdom that comes down from above, but is earthly, unspiritual, demonic. For where jealousy and selfish ambition exist, there will be disorder and every vile practice. But the wisdom from above is first pure, then peaceable, gentle, open to reason, full of mercy and good fruits, impartial and sincere. And a harvest of righteousness is sown in peace by those who make peace. (Jas 3.13–18)

It's not always easy. At times, it's downright inconvenient. It may go against every impulse that screams from within. But men of integrity think before they act. Men of character ask the tough questions. What's my motivation? Am I being true to my Father's expectations? Would wisdom dictate the fulfillment of my impulses? Will my actions lead to peace or only fuel further disorder?

Immanuel, man as God envisioned, set the standard of his

kingdom long ago when he said, "Blessed are the peacemakers, for they shall be called sons of God" (Matt 5.9). No one ever made peace by acting without thinking.

When People Try to Help Us, It's Time to Shut Up and Listen

> Faithful are the wounds of a friend. ...Oil and perfume make the heart glad, so a man's counsel is sweet to his friend. ...Iron sharpens iron, so one man sharpens another. (Prov 27.6, 9, 17)

When our emotions have gotten the best of us, the last thing we may want to do is listen to the objective counsel or pointed rebuke of a friend. In fact, the Enemy would prompt us in a completely different direction. Our flesh is all too eager to promote excuses and rationalizations. "What does he know anyway? If she were really my friend, she would support me. He's just going along with the other guy to get something out of it. She doesn't even understand what I'm going through."

We entertain such thoughts of selfish ambition long enough and we quickly find ourselves occupying the position of the fool.

> Fools despise wisdom and instruction. (Prov 1.7)

> Whoever corrects a scoffer gets himself abuse, and he who reproves a wicked man incurs injury. Do not reprove a scoffer, or he will hate you. (Prov 9.7–8)

> The wise of heart will receive commandments, but a babbling fool will come to ruin. (Prov 10.8)

> A fool takes no pleasure in understanding, but only in expressing his opinion. (Prov 18.2)

> A fool's lips walk into a fight, and his mouth invites a beating. A fool's mouth is his ruin, and his lips are a snare to his soul. (Prov 18.6–7)

> A fool gives full vent to his spirit, but a wise man quietly holds it back. (Prov 29.11)

The man of integrity is willing to recognize, however personally painful that recognition may be, that he doesn't have all of the answers. At times he's made false assumptions. He's prone to jumping to conclusions and losing his temper. Nothing is gained from stubbornness. He's not doing himself any favors when he snaps at a faithful friend who is simply making an effort to discern the ways of truth and righteousness.

To David's very great credit, his sword was in his hand, his horse was out of breath from the anger-fueled charge and four hundred men were ready for a slaughter at his command, but he stopped long enough to listen to a discerning woman who was only trying to help. "The way of a fool is right in his own eyes, but a wise man listens to advice" (Prov 12.15).

Real Men Are Willing to Admit When They're Wrong

How foolish when a spouse, a parent, a child or a friend is only trying to help us because they love us and we bullheadedly continue on the offensive—perhaps even redirecting our wrath toward the wholly innocent—because we're too stubborn to admit when we're wrong. Those who love us must periodically hold up the mirror of God's truth so that we can get a good look at ourselves. Once again, listen to James' description of the bullheaded fool: "[He] looks at himself and goes away and at once forgets what he was like. But the one who looks into the perfect law, the law of liberty, and perseveres, being no hearer who forgets but a doer who acts, he will be blessed in his doing" (Jas 1.24–25).

Our Creator is intent on molding us according to the law of liberty. Regardless of our past, we can be set free! Like the saints in first-century Colosse, our own corrupting shackles of "anger, wrath and malice" can be broken. "In these you too once walked, when you were living in them. But now you must put them all away" (Col 3.7–8). We know all too well what it is to walk those trails, but we also are called to grow up and leave them behind for the higher roads of integrity.

Thank God that just as the early church was blessed with "the apostles, the prophets, the evangelists, the shepherds and teachers" for the "building up of the body of Christ" (Eph 4.11–12), so we also are blessed with brothers and sisters in Christ, friends and family members who lovingly hold up the mirror of truth in an effort to correct us. Who in his right mind would pluck out his eyeball because it enabled him to see how close to the edge of a cliff he was standing? What sane person would cut off his ear because it was annoying to hear the train approaching as he stood in its tracks? And why would we ignore or lash out at those who care for our souls to the point of reproving us when we need it?

In spite of the passions that at times got him into trouble, David was a man after God's own heart. He was a man of integrity. "A soft answer" has the unrivaled power to "turn away wrath," (Prov 15.1), and David was mature enough to listen to such an answer and admit when he was wrong. Immediately after Abigail's reasoned appeal, David replied, "Blessed be the LORD, the God of Israel, who sent you this day to meet me! Blessed be your discretion, and blessed be you, who have kept me this day from bloodguilt and from avenging myself with my own hand!" (1 Sam 25.32–33).

To paraphrase, "Thank you. Thanks to Jehovah for sending you my way. Thank you for your wisdom and tact. Thank you for standing up and telling me what I needed to hear. Thank you for helping me when I needed it the most, but couldn't see it. You've helped me to be a better man." May God bless each of us with faithful friends who are willing to wound us because they love us, and may he grant us eyes to see when the sparks of iron striking iron are flying for our own good.

The Righteous Judge Will One Day Right All Wrongs

We've noted David's thankfulness for not avenging himself with his own hand, but we've yet to note the end of the story.

> And Abigail came to Nabal, and behold, he was holding a feast in his house, like the feast of a king. And Nabal's heart was merry within him, for he was very drunk. So she told him nothing at all until the morning light. In the morning, when the wine had gone out of Nabal, his wife told him these things, and his heart died within him, and he became as a stone. And about ten days later the LORD struck Nabal, and he died.
>
> When David heard that Nabal was dead, he said, "Blessed be

the Lord who has avenged the insult I received at the hand of
Nabal, and has kept back his servant from wrongdoing. The Lord
has returned the evil of Nabal on his own head." Then David sent
and spoke to Abigail, to take her as his wife. …She followed the
messengers of David and became his wife. (1 Sam 25.36–42)

We are the recipients of a promise. We will not always understand why. At times, there may be no detectable sense of justice. The means will remain a mystery, but the promise stands.
"God will bring every deed into judgment, with every secret thing,
whether good or evil" (Ecc 12.14). God's Son "learned obedience through what he suffered" (Heb 5.8) and "kept entrusting
Himself to Him who judges righteously" (1 Pet 2.23, NASB). As
our King, he's personally been through the fire and his marching
orders for every soldier of integrity are clear.

> Do not say, "I will repay evil"; wait for the Lord, and he will
> deliver you. (Prov 20.22)

> Bless those who persecute you; bless and do not curse them.
> …Live in harmony with one another. …Repay no one evil for
> evil, but give thought to do what is honorable in the sight of
> all. If possible, so far as it depends on you, live peaceably with
> all. Beloved, never avenge yourselves, but leave it to the wrath of
> God, for it is written, "Vengeance is mine, I will repay, says the
> Lord." To the contrary, "if your enemy is hungry, feed him; if he
> is thirsty, give him something to drink; for by so doing you will
> heap burning coals on his head." Do not be overcome by evil, but
> overcome evil with good. (Rom 12.14–21)

> See that no one repays anyone evil for evil, but always seek to do
> good to one another and to everyone. (1 Thes 5.15)

> Do not repay evil for evil or reviling for reviling, but on the con-
> trary, bless, for to this you were called, that you may obtain a
> blessing. (1 Pet 3.9)

To this you were called—the pathway of integrity, the trail our
Savior has blazed. As we make our way, the going will at times
be tough. Tempers will flare, insults will be hurled, bitterness will

simmer, revenge will be sought, and battle lines will be drawn, but such will characterize the doomed camp of the Enemy.

> Now the works of the flesh are evident: sexual immorality, impurity, sensuality, idolatry, sorcery, enmity, strife, jealousy, fits of anger, rivalries, dissensions, divisions, envy, drunkenness, orgies, and things like these. I warn you, as I warned you before, that those who do such things will not inherit the kingdom of God. (Gal 5.19–21)

In the victorious camp of the King, the story is different. Strength is needed. Discernment is vital. Open ears are helpful. A calm spirit is indispensable. Let's make sure that when the bullets of anger begin to fly and the bombs of wrath begin to explode, we make our King proud.

10

Sins of the Tongue
Loose Lips Sink Ships

When there are many words, transgression is unavoidable, but he who restrains his lips is wise. (Prov 10.19, NASB)

During the second World War, millions of ordinary citizens volunteered or were drafted as soldiers for the United States Army. Most had no concept of the danger that "loose lips" posed to the security of their fellow soldiers abroad. An innocent conversation about where your company was headed might lead to a massacre. A casual comment on the location of a battleship carrying your buddies could produce disaster. Mindless babbling had the dangerous potential to result in bloodshed.

In an effort to curb the potential for catastrophe, the U.S. Office of War Information launched a nation-wide campaign whereby soldiers and civilians alike were constantly reminded of the need to limit talk of military equipment, troop movements and convoy positions. "If you tell where he's going, he may never get there!" "Americans suffer when careless talk kills!" "Loose lips sink ships!" These and other simple slogans drove the point home loud and clear. With enemy submarines that could be patrolling anywhere, less talk meant greater security.

But loose lips don't just sink ships. They condemn souls. The field manual of our Lord's army warns each soldier of the danger, and even uses ships as an example.

For we all stumble in many ways, and if anyone does not stumble in what he says, he is a perfect man, able also to bridle his whole body. If we put bits into the mouths of horses so that they obey us, we guide their whole bodies as well. Look at the ships also: though they are so large and are driven by strong winds, they are guided by a very small rudder wherever the will of the pilot directs. So also the tongue is a small member, yet it boasts of great things.

How great a forest is set ablaze by such a small fire! And the tongue is a fire, a world of unrighteousness. The tongue is set among our members, staining the whole body, setting on fire the entire course of life, and set on fire by hell. For every kind of beast and bird, of reptile and sea creature, can be tamed and has been tamed by mankind, but no human being can tame the tongue. It is a restless evil, full of deadly poison. (Jas 3.2–8)

Small but powerful. Useful but dangerous. "Death and life are in the power of the tongue" (Prov 18.21). It can be tactfully employed to stir others to selfless sacrifice and zealous good works, but it can also be abused as a destructive flamethrower, ignited by the fires of hell itself. An entire world of potential unrighteousness resides within this tiny muscle. The secret, however, to bridling the beast within has little to do with placing leather straps inside of one's mouth and everything to do with restraining what comes in and out of the heart. What is the rudder that guides the direction of every man's tongue? The mechanism is the mind.

The Mind behind the Muscle

James goes on to mention a number of areas in which our mouths repeatedly get us into trouble: bitter jealousy, selfish ambition, arrogance, lying, fighting, quarreling, conflicts. Then, a simple question.

Who among you is wise and understanding? Let him show by his good behavior his deeds in the gentleness of wisdom. ...The wisdom from above is first pure, then peaceable, gentle, reasonable, full of mercy and good fruits, unwavering, without hypocrisy. ...Cleanse your hands, you sinners; and purify your hearts, you double-minded. (Jas 3.13, 17; 4.8, NASB)

Grasp the point. The problem is not inherent to the muscle in your mouth. The trouble comes from an unfiltered mind. Allow yourself to seethe with anger or bitterness and the torch of the tongue is kindled. Welcome thoughts of lust or selfishness and flames begin to fly. Fuel the fire with pride or arrogance and the great forest of your life can be set ablaze. It's virtually impossible to inwardly fan the sparks of these sinful passions and simultaneously avoid expressing ourselves in an ungodly way with our mouths.

Behind your teeth rests a lethal weapon full of venomous poison. Most critical of all, beyond the toxic flamethrower is a sinfully divided heart.

> With it we bless our Lord and Father, and with it we curse people who are made in the likeness of God. From the same mouth come blessing and cursing. My brothers, these things ought not to be so. Does a spring pour forth from the same opening both fresh and salt water? Can a fig tree, my brothers, bear olives, or a grapevine produce figs? Neither can a salt pond yield fresh water. (Jas 3.9–12)

Do you remember our definition of *integrity* from Chapter 3? "Steadfast adherence to a strict moral or ethical code; the state of being unimpaired; soundness; the quality or condition of being whole or undivided; completeness." That's integrity. It's the very opposite of hypocrisy, and it's the only pathway to the presence of God.

> O LORD, who shall sojourn in your tent?
>   Who shall dwell on your holy hill?
> He who walks blamelessly and does what is right
>   And speaks truth in his heart;
> Who does not slander with his tongue
>   And does no evil to his neighbor,
>   Nor takes up a reproach against his friend. (Psa 15.1–3)

James has warned us of operating according to a double standard in the use of our mouths. The psalmist has pointed out that the trail of the Creator can only be traveled by men of full devotion and true character. Notice that he has also described the camp of the Enemy in Psalm 12.2–4:

Everyone utters lies to his neighbor;
> With flattering lips and a double heart they speak.

May the LORD cut off all flattering lips,
> The tongue that makes great boasts,

Those who say, "With our tongue we will prevail,
> Our lips are with us; who is master over us?"

Not so for the men of character who make up the camp of the King. They are soldiers of wholehearted integrity. Their hearts have been yielded to the Father as tablets for divine engraving.

The words of the LORD are pure words,
> Like silver refined in a furnace on the ground,
> Purified seven times. (Psa 12.6)

The Rotten Fruit that Sprouts from a Corrupt Heart

"No good tree bears bad fruit, nor does a bad tree bear good fruit. Each tree is recognized by its own fruit. People do not pick figs from thornbushes, or grapes from briers. The good man brings good things out of the good stored up in his heart, and the evil man brings evil things out of the evil stored up in his heart. For out of the overflow of his heart his mouth speaks." (Luke 6.43–45, NIV)

Taking the Name of the Lord in Vain

"Blessed be your glorious name, which is exalted above all blessing and praise" (Neh 9.5). "O LORD, our Lord, how majestic is your name in all the earth!" (Psa 8.1). "Holy and awesome is his name" (Psa 111.9). "Our Father in heaven, hallowed be your name," or, as the New Living Translation puts it, "May your name be honored" (Matt 6.9). Isn't the point clear? The name of our Creator is exceptional. As the Almighty, he has every right to express his expectation that we would esteem his name with humble reverence and respect. In fact, the third of the ten basic commandments to Israel was "You shall not take the name of the LORD your God in vain, for the LORD will not hold him guiltless who takes his name in vain" (Exod 20.7).

It is here that we discover the very idea behind our often used and seldom understood word, "profanity." From the Latin *profanum*, the term literally means "outside the Temple." The ground outside of the Temple was free to be used in any number of lawful ways. However, the ground within the Temple was to be regarded as holy, hallowed, and sacred. Treating the Temple grounds as if they were a completely ordinary plot of land would be to profane that which God had sanctified. Entering into the Temple as if it were nothing more than a common complex would be to blaspheme that which God had consecrated.

Building on that point, when I take the name of the Lord in vain, I'm guilty of reckless, irreverent profanity. Who do I think I am when I use the esteemed name of God in a phrase of condemnation? How much more disrespectful could I be than when I call upon the Creator to damn someone or something? Thousands of years ago, our awesome God exclaimed, "my name is blasphemed continually every day" (Isa 52.5, NKJV). But have times changed when his name is used to curse everything from a missed free-throw to a precious soul? Such is profanity, and it will not be tolerated by our holy King.

Furthermore, while I might refrain from using my Father's name in a curse, am I not still typifying the loosest of lips when I use his holy name as if it were nothing more than an exclamation point? When "Oh my God!" is used in the most flippant of ways, am I not guilty of irresponsible disrespect? When I use a wonderful phrase like "Praise the Lord!" in completely meaningless contexts, am I not guilty of careless irreverence?

"You are a chosen race, a royal priesthood, a holy nation, a people for his own possession, that you may proclaim the excellencies of him who called you out of darkness into his marvelous light" (1 Pet 2.9). We have come to naturally expect disrespectful profanity from those still enslaved by the powers of darkness. We hear it at work, on television, at school. We hear it everywhere. But we must not hear it from the mouths of God's holy nation. "As he who called you is holy, you also be holy in all your conduct" (1 Pet 1.15).

Lying

"What man is there who desires life and loves many days, that he may see good? Keep your tongue from evil and your lips from speaking deceit" (Psa 34.12–13). Men of integrity make up their minds, just as Job did. "As long as my breath is in me, and the spirit of God is in my nostrils, my lips will not speak falsehood, and my tongue will not utter deceit … till I die I will not put away my integrity from me" (Job 27.3–5). The point is plain. Your integrity (or lack thereof) will be revealed by whether or not you are a person of honesty. When you use your mouth to deceive, you lay down your honor. "You give your mouth free rein for evil, and your tongue frames deceit" (Psa 50.19).

Of the seven things listed in Proverbs 6 that our God hates, how significant that two revolve around lying. The Lord loathes lying. We shouldn't be surprised, then, at the lack of any mystery attached to the destiny of the deceitful. "All liars shall have their part in the lake which burns with fire and brimstone, which is the second death" (Rev 21.8, NKJV).

Have you made up your mind? Are you determined to be a faithful image-bearer? If so, "Do not lie to one another, seeing that you have put off the old self with its practices and have put on the new self, which is being renewed in knowledge after the image of its creator" (Col 3.9–10). Enough said.

Flattery

In Psalm 5.9, David described men with "no truth in their mouth; their inmost self is destruction." They are not who they claim to be. They are not as dependable or trustworthy as initially thought. Though they may appear to be outwardly cordial and helpful, there is nothing reliable in what they say. Why? Beneath the surface, seeds of corruption have been allowed to take root. As a result, "Their throat is an open grave; they flatter with their tongue."

What's the big deal with flattery? The fact that it's defined as "insincere praise"—the very opposite approach of the man of integrity who is determined to use his mouth in an honest and transparent way. If he says it, he means it. He will not use his tongue as a deceitful cloak to build up while inwardly plotting to tear down. His "yes" means yes. His "no" means no.

Perhaps as a business man, a factory worker, or a college student you can relate to the lament of David in Psalm 12.2: "Everyone utters lies to his neighbor; with flattering lips and a double heart they speak." The consistent connection between the counterfeit use of one's mouth and an insincere heart is hard to miss, isn't it? The overflow of what resides in the heart will produce the substance of speech.

Paul's warning to first-century saints in Rome continues to be urgent and relevant.

> I appeal to you, brothers, to watch out for those who cause divisions and create obstacles contrary to the doctrine that you have been taught; avoid them. For such persons do not serve our Lord Christ, but their own appetites, and by smooth talk and flattery they deceive the hearts of the naive. (Rom 16.17–18)

Divisions. Obstacles. That which is contrary to what God has revealed. Self-gratification. Deception. These are the tactics of our Enemy. They are as old as Eve's conversation with the serpent in Eden. They are indulgently used in all spheres of human existence. But they are unacceptable in the ranks of the redeemed.

Boasting

David's prayer was that "the LORD cut off all flattering lips, the tongue that makes great boasts, those who say, 'With our tongue we will prevail, our lips are with us; who is master over us?'" (Psa 12.3–4).

In what do you boast? Are you a bragger? Is the bulk of the praise which comes from your mouth aimed at self-exaltation?

In Isaiah 10.12–15, the Lord turned his attention to "the speech of the arrogant heart of the king of Assyria and the boastful look in his eyes." In his overconfidence, the king had reasoned:

> "By the strength of my hand I have done it, and by my wisdom, for I have understanding; I remove the boundaries of peoples, and plunder their treasures; like a bull I bring down those who

sit on thrones. My hand has found like a nest the wealth of the peoples; and as one gathers eggs that have been forsaken, so I have gathered all the earth; and there was none that moved a wing or opened the mouth or chirped."

Listen to the logical answer of the Creator in response. "Shall the axe boast over him who hews with it, or the saw magnify itself against him who wields it? As if a rod should wield him who lifts it, or as if a staff should lift him who is not wood!" Such is foolishness and the very definition of ignorance.

To the man who can't get his eyes off of himself, the Almighty says,

> "Let not the wise man boast in his wisdom, let not the mighty man boast in his might, let not the rich man boast in his riches, but let him who boasts boast in this, that he understands and knows me, that I am the LORD who practices steadfast love, justice and righteousness in the earth. For in these things I delight, declares the LORD." (Jer 9.23–24)

You can delight in yourself all day, every day, for the rest of your life. You can boast in your own inconsequential accomplishments and accolades until you have no more breath. But fail to delight the Lord in the way that you talk because of the self-centeredness and arrogance that fills your heart and you will have missed the very reason for which you were created.

The tongue is a small member that boasts of great things, but when it does, it reveals just how small the man behind the tongue really is. "Let the one who boasts, boast in the Lord. For it is not the one who commends himself who is approved, but the one whom the Lord commends" (2 Cor 10.17–18).

Slander

"O LORD, who shall sojourn in your tent? Who shall dwell on your holy hill? He who walks blamelessly and does what is right and speaks truth in his heart; who does not slander with his tongue and does no evil to his neighbor, nor takes up a reproach against his friend" (Psa 15.1–3).

"Do not speak evil against one another, brothers. The one who speaks against a brother or judges his brother, speaks evil against the law and judges the law" (Jas 4.11–12). More than a dozen times throughout the New Testament the disciple of Christ is warned about using the tongue as a weapon of slander. Slander is character assassination. It's an attempt to smear the reputation of someone else. Backstabbing, backbiting, gossip and whispering are all words associated with slander—a scornful and insolent determination to use the mouth God gave us to hurt someone else.

Our Lord was slandered after irrefutably casting out a demon from a mute man. "The crowds marveled, saying, 'Never was anything like this seen in Israel.' But the Pharisees said, 'He casts out demons by the prince of demons'" (Matt 9.32–34). They couldn't disprove what he had done, but they could badmouth his reputation. Their smear campaign continued in Matthew 12.23–24: "All the people were amazed, and said, 'Can this be the Son of David?' But when the Pharisees heard it, they said, 'It is only by Beelzebul, the prince of demons, that this man casts out demons.'" They couldn't refute his power, but they could malign his motives.

Do you remember Jesus' promise in John 15?

> "If the world hates you, know that it has hated me before it hated you. …Remember the word that I said to you: 'A servant is not greater than his master.' If they persecuted me, they will also persecute you. …But all these things they will do to you on account of my name, because they do not know him who sent me." (John 15.18–21)

Our King has already told us to expect the artillery of slander to be fired from Satan's camp. The Adversary is aptly described as the great "accuser" of God's people in Revelation 12.10. Those under his sway are characterized by "an unhealthy craving for controversy and for quarrels about words which produce envy, dissension, slander, evil suspicions, and constant friction among people who are depraved of the truth" (1 Tim 6.4–5).

In fact, our English word *slander* is most frequently translated from one of two Greek words. The first is *blasphemia*, which means to speak against the good character of someone—in this case, one who bears the image of God. Remember how James described the tongue as a "restless evil, full of deadly poison. With it we bless our Lord and Father, and with it we curse people who are made in the likeness of God" (Jas 3.8–9). Such is a form of blasphemy.

The second word is *diabolos*, a word used to identify the devil himself. This is exactly where Jesus took the issue in John 8.44:

> "You are of your father the devil, and your will is to do your father's desires. He was a murderer from the beginning, and has nothing to do with the truth, because there is no truth in him. When he lies, he speaks out of his own character, for he is a liar and the father of lies."

We couple Jesus' words in John 8.44 with his warning in Matthew 15.19 and we find Satan's blueprint for the soul's destruction clearly laid out before us: "For out of the heart come evil thoughts, murder, adultery, sexual immorality, theft, false witness, slander" (Jas 3.10a).

Here is the artillery engineered by the Enemy. If I don't diligently defend the high ground of my mind from anger, malice, hatred, bitterness, jealousy, deceit and hypocrisy, my tongue will eventually become a willing instrument to express the ill will of a corrupt heart. I will march in step with those who grieved the soul of David as he wrote Psalm 57.4. "My soul is in the midst of lions; I lie down amid fiery beasts—the children of man, whose teeth are spears and arrows, whose tongues are sharp swords."

"My brothers, these things ought not to be so" (James 3.10b).

Complaining and Grumbling

"In everything you do, stay away from complaining and arguing, so that no one can speak a word of blame against you" (Phil 2.14, NLT). Have you ever tried to keep track of how much complaining you do in the span of just one day? Many of us are quite effective at mirroring Job's attitude—"I will not restrain my mouth; I will speak in the anguish of my spirit; I will complain in the bitterness of my soul" (Job 7.11)—while living in the "lap of luxury" when compared to Job.

As a soldier aiming at a life of integrity, take the challenge issued by Paul in Philippians 2 seriously. The next time you feel like complaining about your spouse, remember that she didn't just get shipped overseas with the military. The next time you feel like complaining about your children, remember that some people would give anything to hear a child of their own crying. The next time you feel like complaining about your car, remember that if you have a car, you're among the most well-off people on the planet. The next time you feel like complaining about your house, remember that unlike some, you know where you'll be sleeping tonight. The next time you feel like complaining about the members of your local church, remember that some Christians around the world can't begin to imagine what it would be like to spend a first day of the week with dozens of brothers and sisters at once. The next time you feel like complaining about the weather, remember that some people didn't live to see what kind of weather today would hold. The next time you feel like complaining about something really serious—like traffic on the highway—remember that some people are dealing with stuff like bombs and bullets today.

A basic study of the wilderness wanderings of Israel under Moses can be summarized in one word—complaining.

> And the people grumbled against Moses, saying, "What shall we drink?" (Exod 15.24)

> And the whole congregation of the people of Israel grumbled against Moses and Aaron in the wilderness, and the people of Israel said to them, "Would that we had died by the hand of the LORD in the land of Egypt, when we sat by the meat pots and ate bread to the full, for you have brought us out into this wilderness to kill this whole assembly with hunger." (Exod 16.2–3)

> The people grumbled against Moses and said, "Why did you bring us up out of Egypt, to kill us and our children and our livestock with thirst?" (Exod 17.3)

> And all the people of Israel grumbled against Moses and Aaron.

The whole congregation said to them, "Would that we had died in the land of Egypt! Or would that we had died in this wilderness! Why is the LORD bringing us into this land, to fall by the sword? Our wives and our little ones will become a prey. Would it not be better for us to go back to Egypt?" (Num 14.2–3)

What was the problem? A lack of faith. Immaturity. Selfishness. Impatience. Spiritual nearsightedness. Fleshly tendencies that must be left behind as we make our way to the summit of Mount God.

Why not make up your mind right now? Draw the mental line in the sand. Expect better of yourself and hold yourself accountable to that higher standard. See if you can go twenty-four hours without complaining about anything. "Instead let there be thanksgiving" (Eph 5.4). If you're like most of us, you'll find it pretty challenging, but most of what is truly rewarding comes with real challenges.

Filthy Language and Joking

"An evildoer listens to wicked lips, and a liar gives ear to a mischievous tongue" (Prov 17.4). "Now you must put them all away: anger, wrath, malice, slander, and obscene talk from your mouth" (Col 3.8). How many of us never take the name of the Lord in vain, steer clear of lying, and rarely say bad things about other people, but can't seem to break the chains of obscene figures of speech and jokes? Paul unashamedly establishes the fact that such is "out of place" for the disciple of Christ (Eph 5.4). Think about that inspired phrase because it bears critically practical importance for the soldier of the cross. I cannot promote filthiness and still find myself standing at attention in the ranks of holiness. I cannot revel in obscenity and lewdness without stepping out of line.

In Ephesians 4.29, Paul warns disciples about "unwholesome" (NASB) or "corrupt" (NKJV) language. In Ephesians 5.4, he continues to elaborate by forbidding "filthiness"—the natural overflow of that which is shameful, immoral and wicked. Hearts filled to the brim with obscenity, indecency and nastiness fertilize tongues that produce filthy fruit.

The Christian is to be ashamed of those things! "What fruit were you getting at that time from the things of which you are now ashamed?" (Rom 6.21). In the past, I may have willfully engaged in indecency and been amused by obscenity, but when I became a part of the kingdom of light, I adopted a higher standard. If I'm not ashamed of those things, I have a lingering heart problem. If I'm not thinking about how offensive my off-color words and actions are to others, I'm still promoting things that should have been put away when I became a soldier of the cross. If I'm not embarrassed at that which is disgraceful, I still have progress to make in my sensitivity to the demands of God's holy standard.

To drive the point home, the Holy Spirit has also prohibited "crude joking" (Eph 5.4), a basic and innocent term that literally means "that which turns easily." It's quite similar to our English word "versatility." That doesn't sound bad at all, but you've seen innocent scenarios turn sinful countless times. Someone produces an inappropriate insinuation out of the most bland of conversations. A harmless remark is easily spun into a clever but not-so-clean joke. Many of us find it all too easy to take the lead in guiding perfectly fitting dialogue into the realm of the filthy. We may even take an odd sort of pride in our verbal versatility. And yet, the Spirit's warning stands. "Sexual immorality and all impurity or covetousness must not even be named among you, as is proper among saints" (Eph 5.3). How many of the jokes I've told could only honestly be described as "sexually immoral" or "impure"?

It's certainly important to emphasize that Christians have not been forbidden from joking in general and good-natured humor, but now is the time for honesty. Integrity demands transparency. Is my sense of humor a reflection of the joy and contentment I have as a redeemed child of God, or could it be more accurately described as an overflow of a garbage-filled mind that identifies more closely with this perverted world than the kingdom of heaven?

While it may take a great deal of discipline and correction for most of us, we can do better. We must do better. Let's begin taking more careful note of how easily we use our mouths to scoff at or even promote immorality. We've been redeemed and it's time we start talking—and even joking—like it.

Careless Words

The danger behind loose lips is perhaps best summarized by Jesus' warning in Matthew 12.36–37: "I tell you, on the day of judgment people will give account for every careless word they speak, for by your words you will be justified, and by your words you will be condemned."

How long has it been since you said something you shouldn't have said? If you're like most of us, it was probably earlier today. You wish you could take the words back, but you can't. You were careless, and now there is a cost. Perhaps you've heard the comparison of words with toothpaste—once they're squeezed out, there isn't any way to stuff them back in.

"There is one whose rash words are like sword thrusts, but the tongue of the wise brings healing" (Prov 12.18). The words that come out of our mouths carry meaning. They are an ever-so-brief window into our souls. That's precisely Jesus' point in Matthew 12. Our words will promptly and powerfully reveal our character. Even the most casual of comments can betray the real moral quality of the elements that have taken up residence in our hearts.

The point? Be careful. Learn the wisdom behind the warning of Proverbs 17.27–28:

> Whoever restrains his words has knowledge,
>   and he who has a cool spirit is a man of understanding.
> Even a fool who keeps silent is considered wise;
>   when he closes his lips, he is deemed intelligent.

Conclusion

"Even before a word is on my tongue, behold, O LORD, you know it altogether" (Psa 139.4). "Whoever keeps his mouth and his tongue keeps himself out of trouble" (Prov 21.23). Those two Biblical facts aren't hard to understand, are they?

If it's time to make some improvements, set your heart on making them. "Be doers of the word, and not hearers only, deceiving yourselves" (Jas 1.22). Objectively look into the mirror of God's truth. Pray for wisdom and self-control. Seek accountability from your fellow soldiers that hear the words coming out of your mouth. In humility, work to nurture seeds of righteous indignation at how easily our Adversary hijacks our tongues to fulfill his plans and broadcast his agenda. Man as the Enemy envisions allows his mouth to be "filled with cursing and deceit and oppression; under his tongue are mischief and iniquity" (Psa 10.7).

On the other side of the battlefield, the ancient admonition of Ephesians 5.8–17 continues to ring.

> Walk as children of light (for the fruit of light is found in all that is good and right and true), and try to discern what is pleasing to the Lord. Take no part in the unfruitful works of darkness but instead expose them. For it is shameful even to speak of the things that they do in secret. But when anything is exposed by the light, it becomes visible, for anything that becomes visible is light. Therefore it says,
>
> "Awake, O sleeper,
>   and arise from the dead,
>   and Christ will shine on you."
>
> Look carefully then how you walk, not as unwise but as wise, making the best use of the time, because the days are evil. Therefore do not be foolish, but understand what the will of the Lord is.

Wake up. Realize the stakes. Walk the walk. Start practicing what you're preaching. Be consistent in the use of your mouth. "Let your 'yes' be yes and your 'no' be no, so that you may not fall under condemnation" (Jas 5.12). Be kind with your words. Commend knowledge by the wise wielding of your tongue (Prov 15.2). If you raise your voice, may it be only in praise. If you clench your fist, may it be for the purpose of prayer. If you make a demand, may it be first and foremost of yourself. Choose the higher road of integrity.

The battle line has been clearly drawn between true and divided hearts. Just as opposing armies wear different colored uniforms, the soldiers on either side of this conflict are demarcated by the condition of their hearts that dictate the use of their mouths. Loose lips reveal a corrupt heart, and a corrupt heart precedes a condemned soul.

11

Hypocrisy
Wearing the Uniform of Both Sides

"Nothing is covered up that will not be revealed, or hidden that will not be known. Therefore whatever you have said in the dark shall be heard in the light, and what you have whispered in private rooms shall be proclaimed on the housetops." (Luke 12.2–3)

William Alexander. Thomas Conway. Johan DeKalb. Nathanael Greene. Robert Howe. Benjamin Lincoln. Thomas Mifflin. Israel Putnam. Philip John Schuyler. Joseph Spencer. Adam Stephen. John Sullivan. John Thomas. Artemis Ward.

Do you recognize those names? Probably not, unless you're an 18th century history buff. Each of them served as a Major General of the Continental Army during the American Revolutionary War. William Alexander was heralded by one newspaper as "the bravest man in America" at the time. Nathanael Greene was a militia private when the war began—the lowest rank possible; he emerged from the war with a reputation as George Washington's most gifted and dependable officer. Israel Putnam, one of the primary figures at the Battle of Bunker Hill, is believed by many historians to have given the famous order, "Don't fire until you see the whites of their eyes!"

These men and their decisions—some brilliant, others short-sighted and foolish—shaped the course of history. Some of them gave their lives on the battlefield for the principles they held dear.

Others became active in the politics of the infant country that was born following the monumental struggle with Great Britain. Even though the average American of the 21st century may not recognize the names of these men, they left their marks nonetheless.

But here's one name that has endured the test of time—and for all of the wrong reasons. Benedict Arnold. He also was a Major General of the Continental Army. He left his own mark on the history of this country. Even today, his name produces thoughts of treason and betrayal.

A pharmacist and bookseller in New Haven, Connecticut prior to the Revolution, Arnold was ambitious and aggressive. In 1763, he repurchased the family homestead that his father had sold when deeply in debt and resold it a year later for a substantial profit. Using his earnings, Arnold bought three ships and established a lucrative West Indies trade. Tensions were mounting at the time, however, on both sides of the Atlantic. Oppressive taxes levied by the British Parliament were forcing many New England merchants out of business. Arnold himself nearly came to personal ruin, falling deeply into debt.

In March of 1775, a group of 65 New Haven residents formed the Governor's Second Company of Connecticut Guards. Arnold was chosen as their captain. By April, he had been appointed colonel in the Massachusetts militia. In May of the same year, Arnold was involved in the successful assaults of three British forts. However, it wasn't long before Colonel Benjamin Hinman arrived bearing orders to assume command with Arnold as his subordinate. Benedict was incensed, feeling unappreciated for his heroic efforts.

Over the course of the next two years, Arnold's devotion to the Revolutionary cause became quite evident. He voluntarily spent considerable time away from his family. He was injured in more than one battle but consistently refused to leave his men behind. At every opportunity he excelled as a leader. Time and again, however, the Continental Congress passed over him for promotion. Politics weighed in just as heavily, if not more than actual military service, and Benedict couldn't catch the break he felt he deserved.

The summer of 1777 marked a turning point, not only in the war, but in Arnold's personal life as well. A series of battles were fought in upper New York that culminated in the American victory at the Battle of Saratoga. Arnold played a decisive role, showing courage, initiative, and military brilliance throughout. News quickly spread that he and his men had single-handedly cut off the British army's attempt to escape in the decisive battle of Bemis Heights. But Arnold received none of the credit he so desperately craved. Bad feelings had existed for some time between Benedict and General Horatio Gates, and even though Arnold had played a vital role in the success of the Colonials, Gates publicly vilified him for exceeding authority and disobeying direct orders.

Embittered and resentful, Arnold threw himself into the social life of Philadelphia, hosting grand parties and falling deeply into debt. Extravagance led to a number of shady financial schemes which only further damaged his reputation. He nearly lost everything when in June of 1779 he was convicted of two misdemeanors and narrowly escaped a court martial.

A break finally came Arnold's way in July of 1780 when he obtained command of the fort at West Point. Benedict, however, had not forgotten the slights of the past. He had already begun a year-long correspondence with the British and eventually offered to hand the fort over for £20,300 and a brigadier's commission. West Point was of strategic importance because the Americans had been using its position to prevent British ships from moving northward and connecting with their forces in Canada—a move that would have split the north from the south and potentially ended the entire Revolution.

Arnold's seditious plans were discovered only when a British messenger was captured on September 23, 1780 with signed documents disclosing the entire plot. Before he could be apprehended, Benedict fled to a British ship waiting for him on the Hudson River. For the next two years he served as a British officer, even leading attacks on American soil.

The British liberally provided for Arnold, but never completely trusted him. He never received the important military command he always felt he deserved. Following the War, Benedict settled in London where he found no job, little admiration, and even some contempt. In the coming years, when confrontation flared between France and England, he applied once again for military service, but suffered only further rejection. Even his shipping ventures eventually failed, and Benedict Arnold died on June 14, 1801, virtually unknown.

On his death bed in Gloucester Place, legend has it that Arnold said, "Let me die in this old uniform (his Colonial colors) in which I fought my battles. May God forgive me for ever having put on another." Though he made an undeniable contribution to American independence, "Benedict Arnold" lives on, centuries later, as an expression used to describe turncoats and traitors.

The Spiritual Benedict Arnold

Surely you see where this is going. As shameful and treacherous it is for a soldier of one of the armies of this world to betray his brothers in arms and don the uniform of the enemy, how eternally more hurtful and devastating when a soldier of the cross forsakes the sanctified robes of the Christ for the colors of Satan. And most dangerous of all? The man who has grown to be quite skilled at and comfortable with wearing both uniforms. If he's around one group of people, he proudly flies the banner of the King of kings. As part of a different crowd, the same man speaks and acts as one firmly entrenched among the ranks of darkness. On Sunday mornings, you couldn't pick him out in the assembly of the saints. But if you saw how he lived behind closed doors, the awful truth would be fully revealed.

We have a word for this sort of betrayal in our English language. Hypocrisy. We refer to those who are guilty of such as "two-faced." They wear different masks, depending on the circumstances. In fact, our word *hypocrisy* actually has roots in the idea of playacting. A *hypokrites* in ancient Greece was "an actor on the stage," a pretender. Today's hypocrite poses as something he is not. He plays his own part in a masquerade which has had willing participants for thousands of years.

David knew how it felt to have two-faced acquaintances.

> For it is not an enemy who taunts me—
>> then I could bear it;
> it is not an adversary who deals insolently with me—
>> then I could hide from him.
> But it is you, a man, my equal,
>> my companion, my familiar friend.
>
> My companion stretched out his hand against his friends;
>> he violated his covenant.
> His speech was smooth as butter,
>> yet war was in his heart;
> his words were softer than oil,
>> yet they were drawn swords. (Psalm 55.12–13, 20–21)

The polar opposite of such hypocrisy is *sincerity*, another word with age-old roots. Fine pottery was a valued commodity in the ancient world and those who were skilled at producing attractive pieces enjoyed a lucrative trade. After skillfully molding a lump of clay into the desired shape, the potter would carefully place his work in an oven to cure. The honest potter would inspect his product after the firing and if any cracks were discovered, the piece would be thrown out and the potter would start over. But in ancient times, as in any age, not all merchants were honest.

The deceitful potter—cutting corners wherever possible— would take a blemished piece, melt some wax, and carefully wedge it between the cracks. After applying some paint over the flaw, the imperfect pieces could then be sold to unsuspecting customers at the price of a perfect product. And what was the natural result? These merchants could sell their wares for cheaper prices, thus undercutting the honest potters.

It was not uncommon, then, to see signs dotting the ancient marketplace with a one word Latin advertisement—*sincerus*. The message? Literally, this merchant sold his products "without wax." His were "sincere" pieces of pottery.

It was within this cultural context that the Spirit of God drew a powerful analogy.

> Now in a great house there are not only vessels of gold and silver but also of wood and clay, some for honorable use, some for dishonorable. Therefore, if anyone cleanses himself from what is dishonorable, he will be a vessel for honorable use, set apart as holy, useful to the master of the house, ready for every good work. (2 Tim 2.20–21)

Who is the potter of the Spirit's analogy? "Now, O Lord, you are our Father; we are the clay, and you are our potter; we are all the work of your hand" (Isa 64.8).

Simply stated, the goal of our Creator is to fashion honorable vessels which are dedicated to the good work of his purposes. And how does he regard the works of his hand when they don't function as "sincere" pieces of divine pottery? Isaiah 29.13–16 contains God's message to those who "draw near with their mouth and honor me with their lips, while their hearts are far from me."

> Ah, you who hide deep from the Lord your counsel,
>> whose deeds are in the dark,
>> and who say, "Who sees us? Who knows us?"
> You turn things upside down!
> Shall the potter be regarded as the clay,
> that the thing made should say of its maker,
>> "He did not make me";
> or the thing formed say of him who formed it,
>> "He has no understanding"?

God knows! There has never been an image-bearer to walk the earth who could hide even his thoughts from God, much less his deeds. When we cover up the blemishes of our lives and act as if God is blind to our hypocrisy, we've turned things upside down. He made us. He knows us better than we know ourselves.

It makes him sick, therefore, when the works of his hands show off the figurative paint of honor and obedience while tolerating the wax of corruption and deceit.

> Bring no more vain offerings;
>> incense is an abomination to me.
> New moon and Sabbath and the calling of convocations—

I cannot endure iniquity and solemn assembly.
Your new moons and your appointed feasts
    my soul hates;
they have become a burden to me;
    I am weary of bearing them.
When you spread out your hands,
    I will hide my eyes from you;
even though you make many prayers,
    I will not listen;
    your hands are full of blood.
Wash yourselves; make yourselves clean;
    remove the evil of your deeds from before my eyes;
cease to do evil,
    learn to do good;
seek justice,
    correct oppression;
bring justice to the fatherless,
    plead the widow's cause. (Isa 1.13–17)

I hate, I despise your feasts,
    and I take no delight in your solemn assemblies.
Even though you offer me your burnt offerings and grain offerings,
    I will not accept them;
and the peace offerings of your fattened animals,
    I will not look upon them.
Take away from me the noise of your songs;
    to the melody of your harps I will not listen.
But let justice roll down like waters,
    and righteousness like an ever-flowing stream. (Amos 5.21–24)

The Potter and The Sunlight

The careful shopper of the ancient world had one means of determining the quality of the potter's work before he made his purchase—hold the pottery up to bright sunlight. As the brilliance of the sun's rays passed through the clay, any flaws beneath the paint could be clearly seen.

And what does the potter of our souls do with the works of his hand? He holds us up to the Son-light. To the saints in Philippi,

Paul wrote:

> This I pray, that your love may abound still more and more in real knowledge and all discernment, so that you may approve the things that are excellent, in order to be sincere and blameless until the day of Christ; having been filled with the fruit of righteousness which comes through Jesus Christ, to the glory and praise of God. (Phil 1.9–11, NASB)

Whereas *sincerus* in Latin literally meant *pure* or *clean* in relation to an added substance like wax, *eilikrineis* in Greek—translated *sincere* from Paul's letter to the Philippian Christians—invokes the idea of the sun's rays. To the Greeks, if something was *sincere*, it had been judged transparently whole and pure by the sunlight.

As has already been established in this spiritual Boot Camp, Jesus of Nazareth is man as God envisioned. He is Immanuel, God with us. "He is the radiance of the glory of God and the exact imprint of his nature" (Heb 1.3). One of his many claims was to be "the light of the world" (John 9.5). It only makes sense, therefore, as the Father seeks to mold men according to his holy vision, that he would lift us up and point us at the Son-light.

> "Beware of the leaven of the Pharisees, which is hypocrisy. Nothing is covered up that will not be revealed, or hidden that will not be known. Therefore whatever you have said in the dark shall be heard in the light, and what you have whispered in private rooms shall be proclaimed on the housetops." (Luke 12.1–3)

Our King has announced that it is time to repent! The day of reckoning continues to approach. Every deed will be brought into judgment, along with every secret thing, whether good or evil. I must take heed. You must take heed. Each one of us has cracked under the pressures of temptation. We've all been scarred by the fires of that great dragon, the ancient serpent who is called the devil and Satan—the deceiver of the whole world (Rev 12.9). The Spirit of God has promised us,

> No temptation has overtaken you that is not common to man. God is faithful, and he will not let you be tempted beyond your

ability, but with the temptation he will also provide the way of escape, that you may be able to endure it. (1 Cor 10.13)

And yet, we have all willfully turned our backs on the way of escape and walked headlong into the fires of the Destroyer of souls. If we say that we have not, "we deceive ourselves, and the truth is not in us. ...If we say we have not sinned, we make [God] a liar, and his word is not in us" (1 John 1.8, 10).

As a result of our own foolish choices, we find ourselves broken and humiliated. Even if our bodies bear no marks of our failures, that which was created in God's image has been fractured. What, then, can be done to repair the ruptures in our souls? Whom can we blame for the depths to which we have sunk but ourselves? "Wretched man that I am! Who will deliver me from this body of death?" (Rom 7.24). As we seek an answer to those questions, we come face to face with two options.

Option 1

We can depend upon the wax of this world. We can ignore the Spirit's warnings and go on vainly maintaining our precious outward appearances. We can search for meaning in materialism, purpose in selfishness, fulfillment in sexual immorality and happiness in idolatry. We can continue to seek, as our highest aim, the applause and admiration of the other sin-fractured vessels around us. But everywhere we turn, we find the warnings of God's perfect Image-Bearer.

> "When you give to the needy, sound no trumpet before you, as the hypocrites do in the synagogues and in the streets, that they may be praised by others. Truly, I say to you, they have received their reward." (Matt 6.2)

> "And when you pray, you must not be like the hypocrites. For they love to stand and pray in the synagogues and at the street corners, that they may be seen by others. Truly, I say to you, they have received their reward." (Matt 6.5)

> "And when you fast, do not look gloomy like the hypocrites, for they disfigure their faces that their fasting may be seen by others.

Truly, I say to you, they have received their reward." (Matt 6.16)

The common thread isn't hard to pick out in those passages, is it? The bright and glossy paint of skin-deep righteous deeds and outward piety may be noticed and even praised by others, but the recognition of men cannot heal the neglected cracks of unrighteousness below the surface. "Beware the leaven of the Pharisees, which is hypocrisy."

> "They preach, but do not practice. They tie up heavy burdens, hard to bear, and lay them on people's shoulders, but they themselves are not willing to move them with their finger. They do all their deeds to be seen by others." (Matt 23.3–5)

> "Woe to you, scribes and Pharisees, hypocrites! For you clean the outside of the cup and the plate, but inside they are full of greed and self-indulgence. You blind Pharisee! First clean the inside of the cup and the plate, that the outside also may be clean." (Matt 23.25–26)

> "Woe to you, scribes and Pharisees, hypocrites! For you are like whitewashed tombs, which outwardly appear beautiful, but within are full of dead people's bones and all uncleanness. So you also outwardly appear righteous to others, but within you are full of hypocrisy and lawlessness." (Matt 23.27–28)

The key element of leaven and its metaphorical use in Jesus' warnings is that it spreads. It doesn't lie dormant. It grows, eventually permeating everything.

The apostle Paul warned young Timothy about those who speak "lies in hypocrisy, having their own consciences seared with a hot iron" (1 Tim 4.2, NKJV). The leaven of hypocrisy can infiltrate and infect us to the point that we're past feeling. We don't even care anymore! We've worn the mask of deceit and uniform of pretense for so long that we no longer experience those pangs of guilt and feelings of remorse. The Message paraphrases Paul's warning in painfully relatable terms—"These liars have lied so well and for so long that they've lost their capacity for truth." Can you think of a more dangerous spiritual state?

Left unchecked to fester, the leaven of hypocrisy quite naturally takes complete advantage of the lusts and whims of the flesh. Every day you allow yourself to function from a foundation of selfishness, it becomes a little easier to do so. Each time the sexual passions of the flesh are sinfully indulged, you feel a little less guilty. Every decision to place the busyness of this world ahead of the kingdom of God makes a little more human sense than the last. Each confrontation born of jealousy and rivalry seems a little more justified. Every outburst of anger and wrath comes a little more naturally. Each slip and abuse of the tongue flows a little more freely. Forfeit your God-given ability to blush and you follow in the ancient footsteps that led to the destruction of Jerusalem.

> "Were they ashamed when they committed abomination?
>> No, they were not at all ashamed;
>> they did not know how to blush.
> Therefore they shall fall among those who fall;
>> at the time that I punish them, they shall be overthrown,"
> says the LORD. (Jer 6.15).

Therefore, our King is calling for swift and decisive action in response to such spiritual infection. The apostle Paul sharply rebuked the Corinthian saints of the first century for allowing an instance of sexual immorality among them to go unaddressed. A man had his father's wife—a kind of immorality that was not tolerated even among pagans—and it was being glossed over by those who had dedicated themselves to holiness.

> You are arrogant! Ought you not rather to mourn? Let him who has done this be removed from among you.
> For though absent in body, I am present in spirit; and as if present, I have already pronounced judgment on the one who did such a thing. When you are assembled in the name of the Lord Jesus and my spirit is present, with the power of our Lord Jesus, you are to deliver this man to Satan for the destruction of the flesh, so that his spirit may be saved in the day of the Lord.
> Your boasting is not good. Do you not know that a little leaven leavens the whole lump? Cleanse out the old leaven that you may

be a new lump, as you really are unleavened. For Christ, our Passover lamb, has been sacrificed. Let us therefore celebrate the festival, not with the old leaven, the leaven of malice and evil, but with the unleavened bread of sincerity and truth. (1 Cor 5.2–8)

Sin had once again infected the ranks of the redeemed. What was the answer? To cover it up? To ignore it? Not for a moment! Drastic measures were prescribed so that the leaven of arrogance and hypocrisy might not spread any further.

Just as then, so also today. Our Creator knows all things. Our greatest attempts to disregard and discount immorality and unrighteousness—as individuals, as families, as a congregation, or as a nation—are more futile than chasing after the wind. To ignore our Father's clear recognition of our sinful cracks and flaws as he holds us up to the light of his countenance is the essence of foolishness and stupidity. "Whoever says 'I know him' but does not keep his commandments is a liar, and the truth is not in him" (1 John 2.4).

The answer to our wretched problem of sin is not found in the wax of this world.

Option 2

The answer is found in the pathways of sincerity and truth. The answer is honesty and transparency. "This is the message we have heard from him and proclaim to you, that God is light, and in him is no darkness at all" (1 John 1.5). In the brilliance of his glory, there are no shadows in which to hide. For the man of integrity, such assurances are not horrifying, but comforting. He has found the ultimate Source of holiness and righteousness, the essence of goodness and truth, the good news of Jesus Christ which calls all men to step "out of darkness into his marvelous light" (1 Pet 2.9).

As obedient children, do not be conformed to the passions of your former ignorance, but as he who called you is holy, you also be holy in all your conduct, since it is written, "You shall be holy, for I am holy." (1 Pet 1.14–16)

There is our target. "The aim of our charge is love that issues from a pure heart and a good conscience and a sincere faith" (1 Tim 1.5). Once again, The Message powerfully paraphrases, "The whole point of what we're urging is simply love—love uncontaminated by self-interest and counterfeit faith, a life open to God."

The man who is living up to the heavenly intention has trained his sights first and foremost on completely opening his life up in love for God. "We love Him because He first loved us" (1 John 4.19, NKJV). By now, we should realize that this love is more than some warm, fuzzy, ethereal experience that makes us feel good while demanding little of us. The loving relationship envisioned by our Creator is manifested in the obedience of his creation. "This is love," John writes, "that we walk according to his commandments" (2 John 6). Any hypocrite can claim to love God, but Jesus' probing question still stands. "Why do you call me 'Lord, Lord,' and not do what I tell you?" (Luke 6.46). The aim of God's Spirit is to produce complete submission to the Creator in the lives of his image-bearers.

One of the natural consequences of such reverent submission is love for God's truth. Unfailing love. Unconditional love. A love for truth even when it hurts. Paul warned of the "wicked deception for those who are perishing, because they refused to love the truth and so be saved." Men who have fallen into this trap have nothing to anticipate but condemnation, because they "did not believe the truth but had pleasure in unrighteousness" (2 Thes 2.10, 12). If the aim of unconditionally loving the revealed truth of my Creator is skewed, I cannot expect to be saved. It is the truth, and only the truth, that can set me free (John 8.32).

"Your word," the psalmist proclaimed, "is a lamp to my feet and a light to my path. ...The unfolding of your words gives light; it imparts understanding to the simple" (Psa 119.105, 130). The man of integrity is willing to recognize when the light of God's truth is exposing personal sin and unfaithfulness. The man of character is willing to open himself up and respond to what Paul described as "godly grief."

As it is, I rejoice, not because you were grieved, but because you were grieved into repenting. For you felt a godly grief, so that you suffered no loss through us.

For godly grief produces a repentance that leads to salvation without regret, whereas worldly grief produces death. For see what earnestness this godly grief has produced in you, but also what eagerness to clear yourselves, what indignation, what fear, what longing, what zeal, what punishment! At every point you have proved yourselves innocent in the matter. (2 Cor 7.9–11)

When a man's aim is unwaveringly centered on love for his heavenly Father and his greatest ambition is to know and live the truth as defined by God's Spirit, the natural result is "a pure heart and a good conscience and a sincere faith" (1 Tim 1.5). Here is where our righteousness begins to exceed that of the scribes and Pharisees of Jesus' day, the hypocrites who gave the outward appearance of righteousness while continuing to maintain wicked and corrupt hearts. To proclaim that you shouldn't murder while harboring feelings of hatred and animosity is hypocrisy (Matt 5.21–26). To preach against adultery while opening up one's heart to lust is deceitful pretense (Matt 5.27–28). Beyond the outward acts of service and piety, Jesus commands us to look within! What's on the inside?

"Either make the tree good and its fruit good, or make the tree bad and its fruit bad, for the tree is known by its fruit. You brood of vipers! How can you speak good, when you are evil? For out of the abundance of the heart the mouth speaks. The good person out of his good treasure brings forth good, and the evil person out of his evil treasure brings forth evil." (Matt 12.33–35)

The question that faces you at this point in the Boot Camp experience is an obvious one. In what condition is your heart? Is it pure? Are you maintaining a good conscience? Is your faith sincere, unfeigned and undisguised?

As the works of the Potter's hands, "If we walk in the light, as he is in the light, we have fellowship with one another, and the blood of Jesus his Son cleanses us from all sin" (1 John 1.7). Nothing but that blood can atone for the fissures of our souls. It's time to leave the wax of this world behind!

As Christians, will we stumble? Of course. Even as redeemed children of light, we have the capacity to disappoint our Creator. "We all, with unveiled face, beholding the glory of the Lord, *are being transformed* into the same image from one degree of glory to another" (2 Cor 3.18).

I am being transformed. You are being transformed. The life of the Christian is a walk. The trials of integrity are a journey. We are each being called to holiness, but if we live long enough, we will each misstep at some point out of cadence with the Spirit's direction. Ask King David. Talk to the apostle Peter.

All the more thanks be to our heavenly Father, then, who has graciously provided for our slips and stumbles. "If we confess our sins, he is faithful and just to forgive us our sins and to cleanse us from all unrighteousness" (1 John 1.9). He knows all too well that we are not perfect, and yet he is unashamed to demand integrity from each one of us. He expects sincerity in our actions. He requires transparency in our motives. He demands honesty when we are wrong.

He is the God who was willing to forgive the sin of adultery when David, as a man of integrity, was willing to cast away the wax of deceit and honestly humble himself in godly grief.

> Purge me with hyssop, and I shall be clean;
>> wash me, and I shall be whiter than snow.
> Let me hear joy and gladness;
>> let the bones that you have broken rejoice.
> Hide your face from my sins,
>> and blot out all my iniquities.
> Create in me a clean heart, O God,
>> and renew a right spirit within me.
> Cast me not away from your presence,
>> and take not your Holy Spirit from me.
> Restore to me the joy of your salvation,
>> and uphold me with a willing spirit. (Psa 51.7–12)

He is the God who was willing to forgive lies, pride and betrayal when Peter, as a man of integrity, was willing to weep in bitterness over his shortcomings, learn from his mistakes, and boldly preach the Messiah's message of self-denial.

He is the God who is willing to forgive you if you will remove the masks of hypocrisy and proudly put on the uniform of King Jesus.

Conclusion

Could the battle lines possibly be drawn more decisively? On one side of the valley of humanity are those who "profess to know God, but they deny him by their works. They are detestable, disobedient, unfit for any good work" (Tit 1.16).

On the opposite side stand the soldiers of the cross. They're far from perfect, but they're forgiven. They continue to show occasional signs of weakness, but they find strength in the grace of God and the encouragement of each other. Their marching orders call for forthright interdependence. "Confess your sins to one another and pray for one another, that you may be healed. The prayer of a righteous person has great power as it is working" (Jas 5.16). They've shed the uniform of pretense for the armor of light. They've removed the two-faced masks and replaced them with the helmet of salvation.

Let us also determine to live and fight and die in the colors of the King of kings. May God forgive us for ever having put on anything else.

Soldiers of Christ, arise
And put your armor on;
Strong in the strength which God supplies
Thru His beloved Son.

Strong in the Lord of hosts
And in His mighty power;
Who in the strength of Jesus trusts
Is more than conqueror.

Stand, then, in His great might,
With all His strength endued;
But take, to arm you for the fight,
The panoply of God.

Leave no unguarded place,
No weakness of the soul;
Take every virtue, every grace,
And fortify the whole.

That having all things done,
And all your conflicts past,
You may o'ercome thru Christ alone,
And stand entire at last.

"Soldiers Of Christ, Arise," Charles Wesley

Part Three

The Lord's Armory

The night is far gone; the day is at hand. So then let us cast off the works of darkness and put on the armor of light.

Romans 13.12

12

Be Strong in the Lord

Depending on the King Who Has Never Lost

Whom have I in heaven but you? And there is nothing on earth that I desire besides you. My flesh and my heart may fail, but God is the strength of my heart and my portion forever. (Psa 73.25–26)

Welcome to the third and final phase of our Boot Camp experience. You've studied the slopes of Mount God, our spiritual Currahee. You've spent valuable time in the Lord's infirmary, seeking the healing that only he can provide. You've carefully studied the landmines planted by Satan on the battlefield of the soul—selfishness, sexual immorality, idolatry, jealousy, anger, sins of the tongue and hypocrisy. As a result, perhaps more than ever before, you sense your weaknesses and inadequacies.

But isn't that the point of any Boot Camp? To break down those who believe they are completely self-sufficient? To instill the perspective that a single soldier is one part of something larger than himself? To tear down the feelings of pride that may cloud a warrior's judgment in the heat of battle? To show just how much progress must be made before men are ready to fight for and effectively defend that in which they believe? To reign in egos and mold them into a willingness to follow the marching orders of a higher authority? That's the path you've traveled to this point. That's been the goal of your Basic Training, but it's time to move on.

At last you humbly and reverently approach the Lord's armory. Like all soldiers of the cross, you're anxious to enter and try your hand at the weapons of holy warfare. But before you do, your attention is directed toward the timeless words etched above this heavenly storehouse.

BE STRONG IN THE LORD
AND IN THE STRENGTH OF HIS MIGHT
Ephesians 6.10

Be strong. A simple and straightforward command. Notice that the Spirit didn't say "look strong" or "act strong." He said, "Be strong."

But how? How can someone who has just passed through "murderer's row" of the works of the flesh and had so many vulnerable personal points exposed possibly determine to "be strong"? Isn't that a similar paradox to telling the person who is grieving to "rejoice in the Lord"? How can one possibly decide to rejoice when he's drowning in the sorrows born of the tribulations of this world? How can you add to your level of strength any more than you can supplement the degree of your joy?

The Heavenly Focal Point

God tells us that the struggle will be won or lost in our minds. On what will we focus? More accurately, on whom? From what source will our joy and strength be drawn?

What better instructor could we have in this final stage of Boot Camp than the apostle Paul? He encourages us to remember the chronicle of his "countless beatings" and how he described himself as "often near death."

> Five times I received at the hands of the Jews the forty lashes less one. Three times I was beaten with rods. Once I was stoned. Three times I was shipwrecked; a night and a day I was adrift at sea; on frequent journeys, in danger from rivers, danger from rob-

bers, danger from my own people, danger from Gentiles, danger in the city, danger in the wilderness, danger at sea, danger from false brothers; in toil and hardship, through many a sleepless night, in hunger and thirst, often without food, in cold and exposure. And, apart from other things, there is the daily pressure on me of my anxiety for all the churches. (2 Cor 11.23–28)

Paul asks us to specifically remember Luke's account from Acts 16 of the good news being brought to European soil in Philippi. He reminds us of a specific Sabbath day. He encourages us to envision the banks of a river, and how he and Silas turned this place of prayer into a place to hear of Jesus. One of the women who heard and believed their message was Lydia. She obeyed the gospel along with the members of her household. But Paul also recounts firsthand what happened as news spread throughout the city of his efforts. He tells of being dragged into the marketplace before the rulers of the people. He details the charges that were brought of disturbing the peace and insurrection against Rome. He shows us the scars from the "many blows" he received with rods. He describes the Philippian prison and what it was like to sit for hours among the common criminals.

Then he reminds us, with a gleam in his eye, of what Luke recorded in Acts 16.25. "About midnight Paul and Silas were praying and singing hymns to God." They had bled from the beatings, but they continued to pray to the God of all comfort. They had been thrown into the innermost prison, and yet they were persistent in singing of the Savior who had set them free.

Does Paul have your attention? Having set the stage, he has us open the pages of his epistle—the one written years after those events in Philippi. The one with specific encouragement for the saints who continued to live in that city. With his own hand he shows us how the Spirit inspired him to saturate his message with calls to rejoice, even as he wrote from another prison cell in Rome.

In every way, whether in pretense or in truth, Christ is proclaimed, and in that I rejoice. (Phil 1.18)

Even if I am to be poured out as a drink offering upon the sacrificial offering of your faith, I am glad and rejoice with you all. Likewise you also should be glad and rejoice with me. (Phil 2.17)

My brothers, rejoice in the Lord. (Phil 3.1)

Rejoice in the Lord always; again I will say, Rejoice. (Phil 4.4)

Notice carefully the qualification in each of Paul's statements. His joy is inseparably linked to his relationship with the Lord. Without this element of truth, such encouragements would be ludicrous at best, impossible at worst. Christ is proclaimed, and in that Paul rejoiced. Even as he was called to suffer physically, if the faith of the saints in God was strengthened, Paul would be glad and rejoice. "Rejoice in the Lord," he tells them. "Rejoice in the Lord always" was his constant encouragement.

Once again, the fundamental question of this phase of Boot Camp is pivotal. On what will you focus? For Paul, the answer to that question was obvious and life-altering. If his focus remained on the shame of the public beatings, despondency would quickly cloud his vision. If all he could see were the iron bars of a prison cell, defeat would inevitably darken his faith. If his happiness and sense of accomplishment hung upon the reception of the hypocritical, hard-hearted people to whom he preached, optimism and hope would indeed be hard to maintain. And yet, Paul consistently spoke of joy. How? His sense of joy was singularly and powerfully drawn from his fellowship with Jesus.

In an intensely personal bit of insight, Paul wrote of "a thorn" which was given him "in the flesh, a messenger of Satan to harass" him.

Three times I pleaded with the Lord about this, that it should leave me. But he said to me, "My grace is sufficient for you, for my power is made perfect in weakness." Therefore I will boast all the more gladly of my weaknesses, so that the power of Christ may rest upon me. For the sake of Christ, then, I am content with weaknesses, insults, hardships, persecutions, and calamities. For when I am weak, then I am strong. (2 Cor 12.7–10)

Paul forcefully charges us to realize what he himself had to learn. Apart from Christ, we can do nothing! The Lord himself has already assured us of such (John 15.5). Like branches severed from a vine, apart from the Source of all meaningful existence, we will wither in spiritual impotence and fruitlessness. On our own, when we are weak, we are weak. In our own strength, when we are lonely, we are lonely. Left to our own devices, when we have been defeated, we are defeated.

But when we turn in humility, away from our determination to pave our own trail, we find the guidance we so desperately need. When we acknowledge our helplessness, we encounter grace. When we confess our weaknesses, we discover strength which comes from beyond ourselves. When we admit our unworthiness, we receive the robes of an heir to the King.

When the power of Christ rests upon us, we are armed with a blessed assurance. In our weaknesses, we are content that he is sufficient. In our insults, we make sure that he is glorified. In our hardships, we rest in the fact that we are not alone. In our persecutions, we rejoice in the hope that his favor is proclaimed. In our calamities, we are made to depend in new ways upon the promise of his strength. "He is not weak in dealing with you, but is powerful among you. For he was crucified in weakness, but lives by the power of God" (2 Cor 13.3–4). Now he offers you a special portion of his strength for the war ahead. His grace continues to be sufficient for the battles of the day. His power continues to be made perfect in the weaknesses of those who seek strength in him. Marching under the banner of the cross, we are empowered and emboldened to profess with Paul,

> I have learned in whatever situation I am to be content. I know how to be brought low, and I know how to abound. In any and every circumstance, I have learned the secret of facing plenty and hunger, abundance and need. I can do all things through him who strengthens me. (Phil 4.13)

You've read of the dangers. You've studied the landmines. You've seen your inadequacies. But have you grown to the point where you will acknowledge your complete and total dependence upon him for survival? Have you been humbled to the point of sharing the sentiment of Charles de Foucauld?

My Father,
I abandon myself to You.
Make of me what You will.
Whatever You make of me,
I thank You.
I am ready for everything,
I accept everything,
Provided that Your will be done in me,
In all Your creatures,
I desire nothing else, Lord.
I put my soul in Your hands,
I give it to you, Lord,
With all the love in my heart,
Because I love You,
And because it is for me a need of love
To give myself,
To put myself in your hands unreservedly,
With infinite trust.
For you are my Father!

Laying Aside The Rags of Pride for The Armor of Light

Perhaps your father in the flesh conditioned you to avoid showing all signs of weakness. Many are the physical fathers who've chastened their sons about showing any degree of vulnerability. Real men, we are told, don't cry. "You can do it. Be strong. Toughen up. Buckle down. Get it done." Legions of the sons of Adam continue to live beneath the guise that as long as they try hard enough, work long enough, push strenuously enough and sweat heavily enough, nothing will get in their way. They can accomplish anything. They can summit any obstacle and defeat any foe.

While those words may sound defiantly strong, living life with such an attitude is akin to walking unarmed into war against Satan wearing nothing but handwoven rags of sackcloth.

For we do not wrestle against flesh and blood, but against the rulers, against the authorities, against the cosmic powers over this present darkness, against the spiritual forces of evil in the heavenly places. (Eph 6.12)

How well will the soldier fare who, clothed in the attire of a peasant, engages the "great red dragon with seven heads and ten horns" (Rev 12.3)? About as well as the man who pridefully wastes his life, believing that he can make it on his own, and forgetting or ignoring the confession of emptiness.

> We are all like an unclean thing,
>   And all our righteousnesses are like filthy rags;
> We all fade as a leaf,
>   And our iniquities, like the wind,
>   Have taken us away. (Isa 64.6)

On our own, we are doomed to fail. With no one but fallible human beings on our side, the battle is lost. Without strength from above, darkness will triumph.

But the Lord of infinite might invites us to cast off the robes of physical pride, acknowledge our weaknesses, triumphantly turn our eyes upon him and humbly say with David, "Blessed be the LORD, my rock, who trains my hands for war, and my fingers for battle; he is my steadfast love and my fortress, my stronghold and my deliverer; my shield and he in whom I take refuge." (Psa 144.1–2)

In his presence, the mountains quake, the rocks melt, the seas flee and the rivers are driven back. The entire universe was produced by the power of his word. His promise is that at the same word, "The heavens will pass away with a roar, and the heavenly bodies will be burned up and dissolved" (2 Pet 3.10). As our Creator, he is unashamed to speak from the whirlwind and place presumptuous human beings in their place.

> Dress for action like a man;
>   I will question you, and you make it known to me.
> Will you even put me in the wrong?
>   Will you condemn me that you may be in the right?
> Have you an arm like God,

and can you thunder with a voice like his?

Adorn yourself with majesty and dignity;
    clothe yourself with glory and splendor.
Pour out the overflowings of your anger,
    and look on everyone who is proud and abase him.
Look on everyone who is proud and bring him low
    and tread down the wicked where they stand.
Hide them all in the dust together;
    bind their faces in the world below.
Then I will also acknowledge to you
    that your own right hand can save you. (Job 40.7–14)

He has put us in our place, but he has not left us on our own.

Come, let us return to the LORD;
    for he has torn us, that he may heal us;
    he has struck us down, and he will bind us up.
After two days he will revive us;
    on the third day he will raise us up,
    that we may live before him.
Let us know; let us press on to know the LORD;
    his going out is sure as the dawn;
he will come to us as the showers,
    as the spring rains that water the earth. (Hos 6.1–3)

Our Father has taken great pains to show us the ugliness of our sins and the hurtfulness of our iniquities. He has clearly revealed the great gulf which exists between himself as the holy Creator and the rebellious human beings who bear his image. His hope is that we would feel godly grief as we honestly reflect on our foolish transgressions. He has torn us for a reason. He has struck us down with a greater purpose in mind. He lovingly and consistently disciplines us that he may heal us and bind us up with the blood of his once slain, now glorified Son. "Weep no more; behold, the Lion of the tribe of Judah, the Root of David, has conquered" (Rev 5.4).

For while we were still weak, at the right time Christ died for the ungodly. For one who scarcely die for a righteous person—though perhaps for a good person one would dare even to die—but God shows his love for us in that while we were still sinners, Christ died for us. Since, therefore, we have now been justified by his blood, much more shall we be saved by him from the wrath of God. (Rom 5.6–9)

Be humbled by and praise our heavenly Father for the "great might that he worked in Christ when he raised him from the dead and seated him at his right hand in the heavenly places" (Eph 1.20). By the same "immeasuarable greatness of his power toward us who believe," we who "were dead in the trespasses and sins" in which we had once walked, "following the course of this world, following the prince of the power of the air, the spirit that is now at work in the sons of disobedience," can be made alive in Christ, forgiven of our sins, and commissioned according to the high calling of God.

What stands between a man and the grace of God? Human pride. Feelings of self-sufficiency. Willful blindness to one's own faults and failures. Our King is not being unreasonable when he demands that we recognize,

> God opposes the proud, but gives grace to the humble. Submit yourselves therefore to God. Resist the devil, and he will flee from you. Draw near to God, and he will draw near to you. Cleanse your hands, you sinners, and purify your hearts, you double-minded. Be wretched and mourn and weep. Let your laughter be turned to mourning and your joy to gloom. Humble yourselves before the Lord, and he will exalt you. (Jas 4.6–10)

The Lord of heaven and earth will draw near to you! That's the promise. In his own ways, in harmony with his own purposes, and in his own time, he will exalt you. The same God who has demonstrated his power in such awesome ways throughout human history has provided you with personal hope. The One "who is able to do far more abundantly beyond all that we ask or think" (Eph 3.20, NASB) has given assurances to you!

And what does he ask in return? The personal realization that the strength which stretches infinitely beyond our wildest imaginations comes only at the cost of saying and meaning, "neverthe-less, not as I will, but as you will" (Matt 26.39).

> Consider him who endured from sinners such hostility against himself, so that you may not grow weary or fainthearted. In your struggle against sin you have not yet resisted to the point of shed-ding your blood. And have you forgotten the exhortation that addresses you as sons?
>
> "My son, do not regard lightly the discipline of the Lord,
>   nor be weary when reproved by him.
> For the Lord disciplines the one he loves,
>   and chastises every son whom he receives."
>
> It is for discipline that you have to endure. God is treating you as sons. For what son is there whom his father does not discipline? If you are left without discipline, in which all have participated, then you are illegitimate children and not sons. Besides this, we have had earthly fathers who disciplined us and we respected them. Shall we not much more be subject to the Father of spirits and live? For they disciplined us for a short time as it seemed best to them, but he disciplines us for our good, that we may share his holiness. For the moment all discipline seems painful rather than pleasant, but later it yields the peaceful fruit of righteousness to those who have been trained by it. (Heb 12.3–11)

What soldier does not fight with greater confidence when he is led by a battle-tested king who has never lost? That is precisely the point! You are a soldier in the army of the glorified King Jesus. Triumphantly clasp his nail-scarred hand. Look into his fiery eyes. Listen to the voice which echoes like the roar of many waters. Do not disbelieve, but believe. Humble yourself in his sight. Joyfully submit to the discipline which can shape you into a redeemed warrior for the kingdom of heaven.

More Than Conquerors

To be "strong in the Lord" is to take the oath of character. To stand "in the strength of his might" is to wholeheartedly engage the force of your God-given will. Genuine discipleship hangs in the balance of your courage and integrity. The rain may fall, the floods may rise and the winds may blow, but faith founded on the Rock of Ages will not collapse. The battle may rage, the temptations may lure and the darkness of this world may be black beyond belief, but the soldier of integrity presses on. He builds and refines his character—one decision, one trial, one temptation, one day at a time.

Faith that overcomes this fallen world is not founded on words like "perhaps," "I suppose," or "I hope." Triumphant trust is established in the Lord and the strength of his might. The soldier of character not only hears the words of God, but he does them. He believes them with all of his heart. Even if it costs him his life, he is ready to give a defense for the hope which drives him. As a result?

> What then shall we say to these things? If God is for us, who can be against us? He who did not spare his own Son but gave him up for us all, how will he not also with him graciously give us all things? Who shall bring any charge against God's elect? It is God who justifies. Who is to condemn? Christ Jesus is the one who died—more than that, who was raised—who is at the right hand of God, who indeed is interceding for us. Who shall separate us from the love of Christ? Shall tribulation, or distress, or persecution, or famine, or nakedness, or danger, or sword? As it is written,
>
> "For your sake we are being killed all the day long;
>   we are regarded as sheep to be slaughtered."
>
> No, in all these things we are more than conquerors through him who loved us. For I am sure that neither death nor life, nor angels nor rulers, nor things present nor things to come, nor powers, nor height nor depth, nor anything else in all creation, will be able to separate us from the love of God in Christ Jesus our Lord. (Rom 8.31–39)

More than conquerors! Leaving behind our pride and unconditionally depending upon the King who has never lost, tribulation leads to trust. Distress enhances devotion. Persecution multiplies perseverance. Famine forges faith. Nakedness builds nearness. Danger produces dedication. Swords shape strength. "When I am weak, then I am strong." Even the artillery of the Enemy which was fashioned to destroy us can be used by our Father for the ultimate good.

We are more than conquerors! As hardships are endured on the battlefield of the soul, we not only triumph in Christ, we construct our character. As sufferings are withstood on the darkest of nights, we not only conquer through Jesus, we broaden our integrity. As the thorns of Satan make us painfully aware of our weaknesses and the frailties of life, we not only claim victory through the power of God, but we glorify him in the process. What more has the Creator asked of his image-bearers than that?

Who Can Be Against Us?

Perhaps an Old Testament example will serve to drive this powerful point home in our minds. In the days of the prophet Elisha, "The king of Syria was warring against Israel" (2 Kgs 6.8). God's spokesman was a thorn of sorts in the side of this foreign king, telling the king of Israel "more than once or twice" of the secret Syrian military plans and how to avoid walking into an ambush.

> And the mind of the king of Syria was greatly troubled because of this thing, and he called his servants and said to them, "Will you not show me who of us is for the king of Israel?" And one of his servants said, "None, my lord, O king; but Elisha, the prophet who is in Israel, tells the king of Israel the words that you speak in your bedroom." And he said, "Go and see where he is, that I may send and seize him." It was told him, "Behold, he is in Dothan." So he sent there horses and chariots and a great army, and they came by night and surrounded the city. (2 Kgs 6.11–14)

Visualize the scene in your mind. Hear the thunder of a great many horses bearing down on this little city. Imagine the gleam reflecting off the mighty Syrian chariots as they approach. Picture the battle-tested army as it completely surrounds the city. They have come to hunt down one man. They know exactly where he is, and even if they have to annihilate a multitude in the process, they intend to eliminate this pesky thorn once and for all.

> When the servant of the man of God rose early in the morning and went out, behold, an army with horses and chariots was all around the city. And the servant said, "Alas, my master! What shall we do?" (2 Kgs 6.15)

It's already too late to run! The city is surrounded. What can one prophet and his lowly servant do in the face of an entire army? Notice how God's oracle responds.

> "Do not be afraid, for those who are with us are more than those who are with them." Then Elisha prayed and said, "O Lord, please open his eyes that he may see." So the Lord opened the eyes of the young man, and he saw, and behold, the mountain was full of horses and chariots of fire all around Elisha. (2 Kgs 6.16–17)

If that doesn't give you goosebumps as a soldier of Christ, I don't know what will! Yes, the battle is hard, but are we not servants of "the King of glory? The Lord, strong and mighty, the Lord, mighty in battle!" (Psa 24.8). "Do not be afraid, for those who are with us are more than those who are with them."

Are fallen image-bearers who are marching in step with Satan being used as a weapon against your faith? Remember the promise of Jeremiah 20.11. "The Lord stands beside me like a great warrior. Before him my persecutors will stumble. They cannot defeat me. They will fail and be thoroughly humiliated. Their dishonor will never be forgotten" (NLT).

Is a distressing brigade of worry encamped around the walls of your life? "Say to those who have an anxious heart, 'Be strong; fear not! Behold, your God will come with vengeance, with the recompense of God. He will come and save you'" (Isa 35.4).

Do you find that the carnal impulses of jealousy and anger continue to be used to bait you into reacting foolishly and out of step with the cadence of integrity? "Be watchful, stand firm in the faith, act like men, be strong. Let all that you do be done in love" (1 Cor 16.13).

Has the Adversary crippled you with fear about actively fulfilling your commission as a soldier of the cross? "Only be strong and very courageous … that you may prosper wherever you go" (Josh 1.7, NKJV).

Are the lusts of your flesh ceaselessly barraging you? Does it feel as if a terrible siege has been laid around the boundaries of your heart? Make the heartfelt words of David your own.

> I sought the LORD, and he answered me
>> and delivered me from all my fears.
> Those who look to him are radiant,
>> and their faces shall never be ashamed.
> This poor man cried, and the LORD heard him
>> and saved him out of all his troubles.
> The angel of the LORD encamps
>> around those who fear him, and delivers them. (Psa 34.4–7)

Do you feel inadequate and unable to accomplish the charge of the King of kings? Humble yourself! Quit trying to do everything on your own. Pray to our Father in heaven, "that according to the riches of his glory he may grant you to be strengthened with power through his Spirit in your inner being" (Eph 3.16).

It is only a question of where you will turn for deliverance. "If God is for us, who can be against us?" With heaven's King on your side, you are in the majority! "I will not be afraid of many thousands of people who have set themselves against me all around" (Psa 3.6).

> For behold, those who are far from you shall perish;
>> you put an end to everyone who is unfaithful to you.
> But for me it is good to be near God;
>> I have made the Lord GOD my refuge,
>> that I may tell of all your works. (Psa 73.27–28)

With God as your refuge, *be strong*. Be mature enough to avoid seeking him only when you need him. Beyond fleeing to the safety and comfort of the Christ in times of crisis, courageously follow him onto to the battlefield where souls are being won and lost.

That field is no place for cowards. There is no place for the cowardly in the kingdom of God. "As for the cowardly, the faithless, the detestable, as for murderers, the sexually immoral, sorcerers, idolaters, and all liars, their portion will be in the lake that burns with fire and sulfur, which is the second death" (Rev 21.8).

"Blessed is the man who trusts in the LORD, whose trust is the LORD" (Jere 17.7). "The wicked flee when no one pursues, but the righteous are bold as a lion" (Prov 28.1). There is no power in this universe that can force you to quit. There is no persecution in this world that can separate you from the love of Christ.

Be strong in the Lord and in the strength of his might. Embrace your calling. Submit to his discipline. Rejoice in his refining. Joyfully welcome his efforts to mold you into the man he has always envisioned. "The one who conquers will have this heritage, and I will be his God and he will be my son" (Rev 21.7).

13

The Armor of Holiness

That You May Be
Able to Withstand in the Evil Day

The LORD has opened his armory and brought out the weapons of his wrath, for the Lord GOD of hosts has a work to do. (Jer 50.25)

The Lord's armory stands before us. We've noted and carefully reflected on the ancient words etched above its door.

BE STRONG IN THE LORD
AND IN THE STRENGTH OF HIS MIGHT
Ephesians 6.10

As we humbly and reverently take our last steps in the Boot Camp of the King of kings, we notice the Holy Spirit's timeless admonition engraved along the walls of the armory's corridor.

The Lord is at hand; do not be anxious about anything, but in everything by prayer and supplication with thanksgiving let your requests be made known to God. And the peace of God, which surpasses all understanding, will guard your hearts and your minds in Christ Jesus. (Phil 4.5–7)

God has very plainly promised to do his part. He is faithful. Not only is salvation from sin and forgiveness of past betrayals available to each image-bearer, but indescribable peace in the midst of future trials is accessible. Even the hearts and minds of the soldiers of the cross can be securely guarded in Jesus. God is faithful.

Now he urges us to what only we can do. Each one must individually determine to be strong in the strength which the Lord supplies. The means provided for fallible men to access and exhibit God's strength is a full suit of spiritual armor forged in the fires of pure and holy glory. "Put on the whole armor of God, that you may be able to stand against the schemes of the devil" (Eph 6.11).

Note carefully the instructions that come with entrance to the armory. God's strength is not some magical force that will somehow mysteriously envelop the warrior of truth. We've not been left the luxury of sitting back and expecting our King to single-handedly deliver us from the Destroyer of men's souls without any effort of our own. We are called to take up God's holy armor and prepare for battle! Now is the time to be on high alert, constantly watching for potential attacks. War has already been declared on each of our spirits. We must answer the call, take up the whole armor of God, find our place in the line of holiness, and courageously engage the spiritual forces of evil.

How foolish to wait for the attacks of the Enemy before we would ever prepare for battle! If we fail, we cannot accuse our Father of failing to stand by us or neglecting to provide for our needs. If we fail, the failure is ours. Our Father has revealed his eternal plan of redemption. His Son has paid the price to free penitent prisoners of war from bondage. The Holy Spirit has led us to the armory of God. Every element that is necessary to overwhelmingly conquer has been made available. We've reached the end of this Boot Camp experience, now it's up to us to put on the armor of light.

> You know the time, that the hour has come for you to wake from sleep. For salvation is nearer to us now than when we first believed. The night is far gone; the day is at hand. So then let us cast off the works of darkness and put on the armor of light. (Rom 13.11–12)

War is upon us. If we wait to prepare, we don't stand a chance.

The Belt of Truth

"Stand therefore, having fastened on the belt of truth" (Eph 6.14). The typical Roman soldier of the first century wore a loose, flowing tunic that was cinched around the waist by a wide leather belt. A soldier's belt served as the foundational piece of his entire panoply, holding his sword in place, supporting him in battle, and binding the rest of his armor together. A leather apron hung from the belt to protect the soldier's abdomen and groin. No soldier would ever willingly press the battle without this piece of armor. To enter into conflict without a belt was to be unarmed, and therefore vulnerable.

So also, no soldier of the cross can successfully engage the present darkness without being supported by and tied together with truth—truth as defined by the Creator. Truth serves as our Field Manual in the battle for the destiny of our souls. Whenever we have lost our way, it is truth that leads us back to the slopes of spiritual Currahee.

> Send out your light and your truth;
> let them guide me.
> Let them lead me to your holy mountain,
> to the place where you live. (Psa 43.3, NLT)

What is truth? Truth is reality as revealed by the God who made us. Truth is irrefutable and irreproachable consecrated fact. It is the truth of Jesus that makes us free to fight in the first place (John 8.32). Truth is powerful. It is solid and impenetrable. "Sanctify them in the truth," was Jesus' prayer for his disciples. "Your word is truth" (John 17.17).

Truth is what ties all of the aspects of spiritual success together. Like the soldier's belt, it is the foundational piece of our armor. God has fashioned, defined, and unveiled truth; our responsibility is to recognize it and fasten it around ourselves so that we might always be reminded to act, talk, and live as men of truth.

> Speaking the truth in love, we are to grow up in every way into him who is the head, into Christ. (Eph 4.15)

Having put away falsehood, let each one of you speak the truth with his neighbor, for we are members one of another. (Eph 4.25)

Let no one deceive you with empty words, for because of these things the wrath of God comes upon the sons of disobedience. (Eph 5.6)

Walk as children of light (for the fruit of light is found in all that is good and right and true), and try to discern what is pleasing to the Lord. Take no part in the unfruitful works of darkness, but instead expose them. (Eph 5.8–11)

The King James Version of the Scriptures translates the Spirit's instructions in Ephesians 6.14 as "having your loins girt about with truth." Historically, such literally had to do with protecting the pelvic region. To "gird the loins" during the Roman Era meant to draw-up and tie the lower garment between one's legs in order to increase mobility and agility. It prevented the loose ends of the tunic from becoming snagged on something or entangled with one's feet. As a soldier, anything that would prevent stumbling or falling down completely was worth the effort.

With those cultural notes in mind, the Spirit's timeless message is plain. Make the effort now to tie up any loose ends that could cause you to stumble or fall in the daily spiritual battle! Be sharp, alert, and ready to respond to temptation with mobility and agility. As Peter instructed, "gird up the loins of your mind" (1 Pet 1.13, KJV). Literally, prepare your mind for action.

Think about it. When and where does all sin begin? Is it when a sinful thought or image first enters our minds, or when we choose to continue thinking on, fantasizing about, and entertaining the sin? The answer lies with the difference between temptation and transgression. Generally speaking, we have little, if any control over the temptations we run across on the battlefield. But we are in complete control of our responses to temptation. We can choose to indulge the sinful passions of the flesh, or we can redirect our minds to the revealed truth of God, just as our King demonstrated. Think back to the devil's temptations of Jesus in the wilderness.

"If you are the Son of God, command these stones to become loaves of bread." But he answered, "It is written…." (Matt 4.4)

"If you are the Son of God, throw yourself down." …Jesus said to him, "Again, it is written…." (Matt 4.6–7)

"All these (the kingdoms of the world and their glory) I will give you, if you will fall down and worship me." Then Jesus said to him, "Be gone, Satan! For it is written…." (Matt 4.8–10)

Jesus' strategy isn't hard to pick out, is it? The fiery darts of the wicked one were met and defeated with the words of truth. The recorded instructions of God and a ready mind of compliance were Jesus' first line of defense.

Now those instructions have been passed to you and me. War is upon us whether we would risk it or not. Temptations will come whether we seek them or not. When they do, the only question is whether the Scriptures will have been wrapped around our hearts to the point that our knowledge of the Creator's intentions will shape our first responses. Or, will we allow the tempter's seductions to lead us away from the ranks of the redeemed? Satan cannot take God's truth away from you, but you can decide to remove it from your thinking.

"Stay dressed for action [literally, Let your loins stay girded] and keep your lamps burning, and be like men who are waiting for their master to come home from the wedding feast, so that they may open the door to him at once when he comes and knocks. Blessed are those servants whom the master finds awake when he comes." (Luke 12.35–37)

Truth has been made available. What a blessing that we can so freely hold it in our hands! Our entire lives can be built upon its foundations. But truth will aid us in the eternal conflict only when it is known. We must study it. We must meditate upon it. We must constantly challenge and evaluate ourselves in its light. We must candidly and transparently apply it. The more time we spend in honest reflection on the truth, the better equipped we will be to fight the battles ahead.

"We do not want you to be uninformed, brothers" (1 Thes 4.13), because being uninformed can cost us everything. At the dawn of every day, prepare yourself to guard and defend the most vulnerable areas of your life. Don't wait for the Enemy's strike in order to prepare for battle. Surround yourself, wrap your mind in God's truth while there is still time!

The Breastplate of Righteousness

The soldier's breastplate protects the upper half of his body, from the neck to the thighs. In the times of Roman rule, breastplates were usually made of rings or plates of brass. Like the scales of a fish, the brass pieces were fastened together so that the armor was flexible in battle, while still guarding the soldier's vital organs from swords, spears, and arrows.

It's no mistake that the Spirit's instruction to "fasten on the belt of truth" is followed by the encouragement to "put on the breastplate of righteousness" (Eph 6.14). In the word of his truth, our Creator has defined that which is right and that which is wrong. He has established the boundaries of what is acceptable and unacceptable for his creation. He has provided wisdom so that his image-bearers might "walk in the way of the good and keep the paths of the righteous" (Prov 2.20). Those paths have been traveled for thousands of years by men of integrity, moral uprightness, holiness, and character. The way of the good is the way of virtue—in quality and in practice.

Remember that our Creator desires to stamp his own image deep on our hearts. His intention is that godliness and integrity would become a natural part of who we are. When we, in humility, allow God to define the standard by which every thing will be measured as "right," we arm ourselves with holy vests that cannot be penetrated by even the strongest of the Enemy's weapons. Once again, Satan cannot rip the breastplate of righteousness from you, but you can decide to rebelliously lay it down and willfully walk into the camp of darkness.

To put on the breastplate of righteousness, therefore, is to dedicate yourself to a life of self-control. Like the soldier who accepts the weight and constraints of bulky armor, the disciple of Christ consents to live within the boundaries of self-denial and submission to God's standard of righteousness. The soldiers of this world do so to protect themselves from the outward dangers of battle. The Christian does so to protect himself from himself.

> Let not sin therefore reign in your mortal body, to make you obey its passions. Do not present your members to sin as instruments for unrighteousness, but present yourselves to God as those who have been brought from death to life, and your members to God as instruments for righteousness. (Rom 6.12–13)

> Little children, let no one deceive you. Whoever practices righteousness is righteous, as he is righteous. Whoever makes a practice of sinning is of the devil, for the devil has been sinning from the beginning. The reason the Son of God appeared was to destroy the works of the devil. No one born of God makes a practice of sinning, for God's seed abides in him, and he cannot keep on sinning because he has been born of God. By this it is evident who are the children of God, and who are the children of the devil: whoever does not practice righteousness is not of God. (1 John 3.7–10)

Just as wicked King Ahab was killed by an arrow that struck him "between the scale armor and the breastplate" (1 Kgs 22.34), a lack of honesty and integrity leaves soldiers of Christ critically exposed to the assaults of Satan. There is no earthly substitute for humble obedience in the sight of God. He expects practical, daily righteousness on the part of the redeemed. He calls us to live in harmony with what is right in his sight. Each image-bearer is summoned to mold his own beliefs, opinions, attitudes, thoughts, and behaviors into a living imitation of the Creator's expectations.

If we are to successfully survive the attacks of the wicked one, we must recognize and address the breaches of personal weakness and compromise. We don't stand a chance against the cosmic powers of darkness while selfishly clinging to the lusts of the flesh. As long as sin reigns in our mortal bodies, there are gaps in our panoply. We may describe ourselves as fully-devoted followers, but we have been deceived. We are continuing to tolerate sin in our lives and the devil has us right where he wants us.

Remember the call! It is time to "cast off the works of darkness and put on the armor of light." Leave no unguarded place! Recognize and address the weaknesses of your character. "Clothe yourselves, all of you, with humility toward one another, for God opposes the proud but gives grace to the humble" (1 Pet 5.5). Seek out the strength which only he can supply. Reform your standards of living so that they reflect his. And having done all, washed in the atoning blood of the Lamb and clothed in accordance with his righteousness, you can resist the advances of Satan, standing firm in your faith.

The Shoes of Readiness

Shoes were an essential element of the Roman soldier's panoply. Equipped with sharp metal spikes beneath, these battle-ready sandals enabled a soldier to walk over all sorts of sloping and slippery terrain quickly and effectively. The Romans prided themselves on their ability to routinely move farther and faster than their enemies. Opposing armies were frequently caught off guard, having deceived themselves into thinking that they had plenty of time to prepare an adequate defense. In fact, more than one historian has noted that the Romans were so overwhelmingly successful as conquerors for so long at least partially because of their superior footwear.

The Spirit uses this familiar figure in his instructions for the soldier of God's kingdom. "As shoes for your feet, having put on the readiness given by the gospel of peace" (Eph 4.15). In contrast to the enemy who is caught barefooted and unaware, the soldier whose feet have been *shod*, or literally, *underbound*, is adequately prepared for battle. So also, our own feet are to be prepared to defend and conquer. Perhaps it would be tempting for a soldier who had endured a long, forced march to leave his belt and breastplate on, but slip his shoes off for a moment of relaxation. Spiritually speaking, God urges us to be always ready. Temptations are relentless. Trials are fierce. The work is neverending. Entire lives can be forever altered in a moment. If the soldier of the cross is unprepared to deal with the triumphs and tragedies of his earthly pilgrimage, he will be defeated.

The sense of readiness which is needed for the battles ahead will not come via our own ingenuity, intellect, or willpower. It is "given by the gospel" or good news "of peace." Remember the divine promise that we ran across as we entered God's armory. "The peace of God, which surpasses all understanding, will guard your hearts and your minds in Christ Jesus." As Christians, we have discovered peace with the holy God. No longer must we run in fear or hide in shame from our Creator. Through the sacrifice of our great King and high priest, we are sanctified children of God who are encouraged to "come boldly to the throne of grace, that we may obtain mercy and find grace to help in time of need" (Heb 4.16, NKJV).

Paul's message to the Ephesian Christians—and to us—is to stand at attention and remain steadfast! Live as men who are grounded in the good news that you are at peace with God. Rejoice in the blessed assurance of forgiveness. Exult in the fulfillment which comes from obedience. Allow your reformed allegiance to reshape your identity. Confidently look forward to the guaranteed glorious triumph. Our Father has pledged that he will never leave us nor forsake us. "So we can confidently say,

'The Lord is my helper;
    I will not fear;
    what can man do to me?'" (Heb 13.6)

Such is the epitome of inner peace. Though the battle may rage in any number of ways all around me, I have dedicated myself to following the Prince of Peace (Isa 9.6). Though I am free from the shackles of sin, I am not free to run in whatever direction I choose. I always remember that I am not my own. As Paul reminded the Christians in Galatia, "You were called to freedom, brothers. Only do not use your freedom as an opportunity for the flesh, but through love serve one another" (Gal 5.13).

As disciples of Jesus, we are to seek the preparation that comes through the gospel of peace. We are to be "ready for every good work" (Tit 3.1). It's one thing to read that commandment, but what does it look like, practically speaking?

> Let love be genuine. Abhor what is evil; hold fast to what is good. Love one another with brotherly affection. Outdo one another in showing honor. Do not be slothful in zeal, be fervent in spirit, serve the Lord. Rejoice in hope, be patient in tribulation, be constant in prayer. Contribute to the needs of the saints and seek to show hospitality.
>
> Bless those who persecute you; bless and do not curse them. Rejoice with those who rejoice, weep with those who weep. Live in harmony with one another. Do not be haughty, but associate with the lowly. Never be wise in your own sight. Repay no one evil for evil, but give thought to do what is honorable in the sight of all. If possible, so far as it depends on you, live peaceably with all. Beloved, never avenge yourselves, but leave it to the wrath of God, for it is written, "Vengeance is mine, I will repay, says the Lord." To the contrary, "if your enemy is hungry, feed him; if he is thirsty, give him something to drink; for by so doing you will heap burning coals on his head." Do not be overcome by evil, but overcome evil with good. (Rom 12.9–21)

That commission is harder to fulfill than storming and securing the beaches of Normandy. If you don't believe that, you need to read it again. It takes preparation. It requires willpower. It demands that my love for the Lord and my fellow man exceed even my love for myself. It's hard. But it's the call of the gospel of peace.

The man of integrity is able to say, "I can rejoice in my Lord always. My reasonableness can be shown to everyone. I can be a peacemaker. I can remember who the real Enemy is. I can respond to anger with kindness. I can endure insults with gentleness. I can react to unjust criticism with mercy and forgiveness. I can walk in peace. My greatest desire is see other people experience the peace of God in their own hearts. I no longer have to be consumed by anxiousness. I can find reasons for thanksgiving in the most difficult of circumstances. In everything, by prayer and supplication, I can make my requests known to my God. Why? How? The peace of God which surpasses all human understanding is guarding my heart and my mind in Christ Jesus. In the power of the glorified Son of God, I can stand firm. Though outwardly the war may rage, inwardly the gospel of peace has securely grounded me in the truth and comfort of my Creator."

Can you honestly say those things as a man of integrity? If not, you have yet to put on the right shoes. You are unprepared for the battle ahead.

The Shield of Faith

"In all circumstances take up the shield of faith, with which you can extinguish all the flaming darts of the evil one" (Eph 6.16). There were two types of Roman shields in the ancient world. One was small and round, designed especially for hand-to-hand combat. The other was much larger, measuring four by two and a half feet, and described in terms more similar to a "door" than a shield. The Spirit commissions the soldier of the cross to take up this latter shield in the defense of his soul.

This shield is solid, designed to protect the whole body. Usually made of light wood, such shields were frequently lined with brass and covered with several folds of thick leather. They could be drenched with water so that as enemy arrows dipped in pitch and set on fire collided with them, the points were blunted and the flames were extinguished. An ancient soldier needed only to kneel down and hold his shield above him, and he would be protected from the flaming barrages of the opposition.

The Spirit tells us that the Christian's shield is forged in the fires of faith. If truth is rock-solid, undeniable fact as revealed by the Creator, faith is unshakeable trust in the Revealer and his revelation. "So faith comes from hearing, and hearing through the word of Christ" (Rom 10.17). God's assurances of things hoped for form our shields. The conviction of things not seen can quench the hottest flames (Heb 11.1).

From a distance we've studied many of the evil one's "flaming darts"—temptations to operate in selfishness, to give in to sexual immorality, idolatry, jealousy, or anger, to lose control of our tongues or to hide behind the masks of hypocrisy. Our Adversary is intent upon our destruction. His own defeat is already certain, but he will use whatever he can to cause fear in our hearts, doubt in our minds, worry during our nights, and rebellion throughout our days. If he can drag us down to the pits of destruction along with him, he will.

But even when this great red dragon blows the hottest fire of his fiercest wrath in our direction, as we stand firm behind the shield of our faith, we have nothing to fear, "For everyone who has been born of God overcomes the world. And this is the victory that has overcome the world—our faith. Who is it that overcomes the world except the one who believes that Jesus is the Son of God?" (1 John 5.4–5).

Temptations will continue to come. Trials will continue to arise. Just because you hold the shield of faith in your hands does not mean that the dragon will give up in his efforts. If anything, his attention is enhanced and his hatred is all the more incensed by those who have been washed in the blood of the Lamb. Like a prowling, roaring lion he continues to seek those whom he can devour. But you can "resist him, firm in your faith, knowing that the same kinds of suffering are being experienced by your brotherhood throughout the world" (1 Pet 5.8–9).

Remember, the devil cannot force you to lay down the shield of your faith. As long as a soldier has his shield, he feels secure. As long as a Christian has his faith, he will overcome. God will deliver him, defend him, vindicate him, provide for him, and ultimately reward him for his faithfulness. But as soon as you choose to lay your shield down, you invite your own devouring.

Don't lay it down! "In all circumstances"—at home, at work, at school, at play, in busyness and in rest, in times of rejoicing and in times of sorrow—hold on to the shield of your faith. You will find nothing else that can extinguish the Evil One's flaming arrows.

The Helmet of Salvation

In the heat of hand-to-hand combat when soldiers fought with clubs, pieces of chain, swords, and axes, helmets that gave secure protection to the head were invaluable. Made of thick leather or brass and capped with plates of metal to cover the temples and forehead, ancient helmets were often ornately decorated with engravings and crowned with a plume or a crest that clearly identified who a soldier was and to whom his allegiance had been pledged.

The soldier who fights for the King of kings is instructed to "take the helmet of salvation" (Eph 6.17). Just as a helmet was accepted by a soldier from the hands of the officer in charge of supply and distribution, salvation is a gift. "For by grace you have been saved through faith. And this is not your own doing; it is the gift of God, not as a result of works, so that no one may boast" (Eph 2.8–9).

As citizens of the kingdom of heaven, we've been reconciled to God through the gift of his Son. We "who once were far off have been brought near by the blood of Christ" (Eph 2.13). The time has come, therefore, to take up the helmet of salvation and unashamedly declare our allegiance to the King. "For freedom Christ has set us free; stand firm therefore, and do not submit again to a yoke of slavery" (Gal 5.1). Turn your back on selfishness. Run away from the darkness of sexual immorality. Renounce idolatry. Reject jealousy and anger. Bridle your tongue and cast off hypocrisy. Hold your head high as you receive your helmet of salvation and advance the cause of holiness with courage. Refuse to remove your helmet! What reason is there to give up when the victory of our God has already been assured?

> Though I walk in the midst of trouble,
>   you preserve my life;
> you stretch out your hand against
>   the wrath of my enemies,
>   and your right hand delivers me.
> The Lord will fulfill his purpose for me;
>   your steadfast love, O Lord, endures forever.
> Do not forsake the work of your hands. (Psa 138.7–8)

The Sword of the Spirit

As we are guided into the last chamber of the Lord's armory, we are shown the only offensive weapon of the Lord's soldier—

"the sword of the Spirit, which is the word of God" (Eph 6.17). In fact, it is both offensive and defensive. It contains the power to defend us against the devil's advances and the potency to force him into retreat. King Jesus demonstrated for his subjects once and for all that when faced with the power of the word of God, the devil must flee. In the light of truth, his words are proven to be lies and his methods are revealed as blasphemous. "For the word of God is living and active, sharper than any two-edged sword, piercing to the division of soul and of spirit, of joints and of marrow, and discerning the thoughts and intentions of the heart" (Heb 4.12).

We have not been asked by our King to enter the battlefield armed with nothing more than our own reasoning and a reliance on our own wisdom. It is only by taking up the sword of the Spirit that we will prevail. It is only by abiding within the doctrine of Christ that we will be secure.

> For though we walk in the flesh, we are not waging war according to the flesh. For the weapons of our warfare are not of the flesh but have divine power to destroy strongholds. We destroy arguments and every lofty opinion raised against the knowledge of God, and take every thought captive to obey Christ. (2 Cor 10.3–5)

It is God's word which destroys the arguments of presumptive men. It is the sword of the Spirit that humbles the lofty opinions of the "wise." It is the sharp dagger of truth that bears the divine energy to prick our guilty consciences, slaughter our self-righteousness, provoke godly sorrow, and spur us on to enslave every aspect of our beings in service to Christ. "All Scripture is breathed out by God and profitable for teaching, for reproof, for correction, and for training in righteousness, that the man of God may be competent, equipped for every good work" (2 Tim 3.16–17).

The skilled swordsman who has courageously engaged the enemy and lived to fight another day knows his sword and how to use it. He studies. He practices. He sharpens his skills long before the next battle ever takes place. Imagine an ignorant and brash man who recklessly storms the battlefield. Why is he ignorant? His only familiarity with a sword is that he's heard other men talk of swords. In what way is he brash? He believes that since a sword has hung for years on his wall that he can suddenly pick one up and effectively use it to fight a war. What a fool! He very well may dismember himself or someone else before ever engaging the enemy.

And yet, how much more foolish is the man who has heard other men talk of God's word, has a copy of the Bible on a shelf at home, has described himself as a Christian for years, but has never learned to effectively use his sword in the service of his King? Ignorance will not defeat the Tempter. Error cannot destroy arguments. Assumptions have little power in the face of tormenting trials. We have no hope of victory if we fail to arm ourselves with truth. The moment we leave God's word behind and begin relying upon our own wisdom and experience, we've doomed ourselves to destruction. It's as if we throw away our sword and decide to fight the great red dragon with our bare hands.

The wise soldier of the cross humbly models Paul's instructions to young Timothy through the disciplines of study, meditation, and prayer. "Do your best to present yourself to God as one approved, a worker who has no need to be ashamed, rightly handling the word of truth" (2 Tim 2.15).

Arming Ourselves in Prayer

The Spirit's instructions concerning the armor of God conclude with the expectation that disciples of Christ would be "praying at all times in the Spirit, with all prayer and supplication" (Eph 6.18). What better way to reinforce heaven's intentions in our minds and dedicate ourselves to the goal of serving as faithful soldiers than to ask for our Father's help and blessing as we reflect on each piece of armor?

Father in heaven, hallowed be your name. May your sovereign rule extend into our hearts and lives. May your will be done in us and through us as it is in heaven. We thank you, Father, for the strength of your might that has been made available to us. We are unworthy even to address you as our Father. We have turned our backs on you in the past. We have rejected the message of your Messiah. But you have not forgotten or given up on us. Even when we were your enemies, you worked to provide a plan for our redemption. We thank you for the blessed privilege of calling on you as redeemed sons.

Blessed Father, we seek your help and blessing as we do our best to recognize the present conflict. Help us to realize the stakes. Grant us the wisdom to feel the weight of the struggle. Guide us in acknowledging our desperate need for your power and patience in our lives. Direct us as we strive to remember who we have been called to struggle against. Guard us from selfish deception that would tempt us to turn unnecessarily on other image-bearers. Lead us to clarity and focus so that you and you alone are glorified in all of our efforts.

Holy Father, we thank you for the belt of truth. We praise you as the Author of reality and the Rock of faithfulness. Send forth your light into our lives. Help us to acknowledge and joyfully respond to your direction. Use whatever you must to guide us to your holy mountain, to the pleasure of your presence. We pray for sanctification through your word and for strength as we strive to be men of truth in your service. Help us to wrap integrity around every aspect of our lives and allow your truth to bind every element of our existence together. We pray that you would help us to stay dressed for holy action, with minds prepared and hearts that are eagerly awaiting the return of your Son.

Righteous Father, we thank you for the breastplate of righteousness. We ask for your guidance as we wage war against sin in our mortal bodies. Help us to cultivate a holy hatred for abusing our members as instruments of unrighteousness. Lead us and be patient with us as we dedicate ourselves as soldiers who have been brought from death to life. Help us to discern your will, delight in your leading, and live as clear representations of your expectations. Guide us as we seek to clothe ourselves with humility. Mold us, Father, to your glory. Purge from our lives whatever you must by whatever means is necessary so that we might glorify you in honesty, uprightness, and integrity.

Merciful Father, we thank you for the shoes of readiness given by the gospel of peace. We magnify you as the great peacemaker in all of history. We praise you for the gift of your Son through whom we can come boldly to the throne of your grace. Help us, Father, to appreciate our freedom. May we avoid using it as an opportunity for the flesh. Guide us that we might be always ready for every good work. Shape us into peacemakers and proclaimers of your good news. Use us in the cause of overcoming evil with good.

Almighty Father, we thank you for the shield of faith. We glorify you for your word which continues to serve as the foundation of our faith. Help us to cling to the promise of victory in the faith that overcomes this world.

Lead us not into temptation, but deliver us from evil. Guard us as we endure the assaults of the evil one. Establish us in steadfastness of faith. In all circumstances, empower us to carry the shield of absolute trust.

Gracious Father, we thank you for the helmet of salvation. We exalt you for your amazing grace. We praise you for the assurance of our relationship with you. We ask for your help as we fight against the urges to submit once again to our former yokes of slavery. Preserve us, Father, deliver us with your mighty right hand. Fulfill your purposes for us and in us. Do not forsake the work of your hands. May your steadfast love, O Lord, endure forever.

Finally, Most High Father, we thank you for the sword of the Spirit, the revelation of your mind and will. May we always appreciate your providence which has made your revelation so freely available. We stand in awe of its living power. Do whatever you must to keep us open to its teaching, sensitive to its reproof, honest with its correction, and receptive of its instructions so that we might be trained in righteousness. Bless our efforts to present ourselves to you as men approved, workers who do not need to be ashamed, rightly handling the sword of your Spirit.

We will follow you, Father, wherever you lead. Whom have we in heaven but you? There is nothing and no one on earth that we desire more than you. Our bodies and our hearts may fail, but you are the strength of our hearts and our refuge forever.

With all of our hearts, souls, and minds, we pledge our allegiance to your Son and our King. Come, Lord Jesus! It is through him that we pray.

Amen.

Conclusion

You have fastened on the belt of truth. You have put on the breastplate of righteousness and the shoes of readiness. You have taken up the shield of faith. You have received your helmet of salvation. Your hand has grasped the hilt of the sword of the Spirit.

Now, as you make your way out of the Lord's armory, you are encouraged one more time to read and meditate upon the words etched above its entrance.

BE STRONG IN THE LORD
AND IN THE STRENGTH OF HIS MIGHT
Ephesians 6.10

Always remember that the pieces of your armor are not trophies of your own triumphs. They are not symbols of your power or signs of your authority. Wearing this panoply is an acknowledgment of your King's grace. It is a testament of your weaknesses and the perfection of his power. It is a triumphant proclamation that echoes throughout the shadows of the present darkness and causes the spiritual forces of evil to tremble. "For the sake of Christ, then, I am content with weaknesses, insults, hardships, persecutions, and calamities. For when I am weak, then I am strong" (2 Cor 12.10).

As you emerge, having been adorned in the armor of light, one thing is clear to the cosmic powers of wickedness. In order to get to you, they must go through Christ! All of the flaming darts in the evil one's arsenal may be launched at you. The strongest temptations and the darkest trials may be desperately hurled in your direction. The assaults of worry, doubt, and fear may be relentless. Every ounce of power that the great red dragon can muster may be unleashed in your life. But as long as you rely on the strength which the Lord supplies, nothing can separate you from him. As long as you refuse to remove the armor of light, you cannot be defeated. As long as you do all in your power to stand firm, you serve on the side that will overwhelmingly conquer.

O men of age, O men of youth,
Lift up your idle swords;
Come fight with us who fight for truth:
The Army of our Lord.

Our Lord sees every Christian die,
And feels each dying breath,
And calls out from a field nearby,
"Be faithful unto death."

Our elders, long in battle years,
Alas, begin to fade;
But from the ranks, young men appear
And lead their first crusade.

Our brethren, dead beneath the plain,
Whose spirits never died,
Rise up to march and shout again,
"O Christ, be glorified!"

"O Christ, be glorified!"

"The Army Of Our Lord," C.A. Roberts

Conclusion

Our Battle Cry

For if anyone thinks he is something, when he is nothing, he deceives himself. (Gal 6.3)

More than two thousand years ago, Cicero wrote, *"Virtute enim ipsa non tam multi praediti esse quam videri volunt."* In English, "Few are those who wish to be endowed with virtue rather than to appear so." Every man wishes to appear as virtuous in the sight of his wife, children, friends, co-workers, and fellow Christians. But not all who seem to be virtuous are so. Therefore, our battle cry, as soldiers of integrity, is *"esse quam videri"*—to be, rather than to appear.

Integrity leads us to live, in the sight of no one, the way we would live if the entire world were watching. It dictates our speech, regardless of who is within earshot. It functions as a filter between our eyes and our minds. It directs our work habits, irrespective of our bosses' attention. It holds us accountable in the ways we treat our wives, both inside and outside the walls of our houses. It serves as a compass for the pathways wherein we will lead our families. It discourages the use of hypocritical uniforms which are taken on and off, depending on the situation. Integrity is being, rather than simply appearing.

Whereas human impressions may often be only skin-deep, integrity is rooted deep within our hearts. And yet, its existence, or lack thereof, cannot be hidden. "You are those who justify yourselves before men," Jesus said to the Pharisees of his day, "but God knows your hearts" (Luke 16.15). The Creator searches each heart (Rom 8.27), and when he finds the image of his Son stamped deeply into a man's character, he rejoices. He has found man as he always envisioned.

> Since we have such a hope, we are very bold, not like Moses, who would put a veil over his face so that the Israelites might not gaze at the outcome of what was being brought to an end. But their minds were hardened. For to this day, when they read the old covenant, that same veil remains unlifted, because only through Christ is it taken away. Yes, to this day whenever Moses is read a veil lies over their hearts. But when one turns to the Lord, the veil is removed. Now the Lord is the Spirit, and where the Spirit of the Lord is, there is freedom. And we all, with unveiled face, beholding the glory of the Lord, are being transformed into the same image from one degree of glory to another. For this comes from the Lord who is the Spirit. (2 Cor 3.12–18)

Every soldier knows that Boot Camp exists in the shadow of oncoming war. Basic training is only the preparatory phase for approaching conflict. You know only a fraction of the struggle which lies before you. There is no neutral ground to be found in the universe. Every inch is claimed by both God and Satan. That is why, when the Spirit tells us to put on the whole armor of God, he uses the language of permanence. As warriors of integrity, we are called to clothe ourselves with God's holy panoply once and for all. The masks we have put on and taken off while playing the games of the past must be set aside. Those who are content with appearing, rather than being, don't stand a chance in the coming fight. The Enemy will conquer. It is not a question of if, but when.

> "Therefore fear the LORD and serve him in sincerity and in faithfulness. Put away the gods that your fathers served ... and serve the LORD. And if it is evil in your eyes to serve the LORD, choose this day whom you will serve." (Josh 24.14–15)

And as you choose, remember. Though the forces of evil are powerful, they cannot defeat the will of the Creator. With allegiance to the Christ comes absolute victory; loyalty to the Enemy brings certain destruction. The outcome of this war has already been decided. As the Spirit of the LORD told Jehoshaphat and his subjects, "Do not be afraid and do not be dismayed at this great horde, for the battle is not yours but God's" (2 Chron 20.15).

As this Boot Camp comes to a close, be honest. Have you made the choice of sincerity and faithfulness? Have you aligned your heart and your life with the ultimate Victor? If not, why take another unprepared, unconsecrated step?

Keep your focus sharp, your courage strong, and your eyes on the King. Perhaps our paths will cross on the field of battle.

> To him who is able to keep you from stumbling and to present you blameless before the presence of his glory with great joy, to the only God, our Savior, through Jesus Christ our Lord, be glory, majesty, dominion, and authority, before all time and now and forever. Amen. (Jude 24–25)

Notes

Preface
[1]George Bernard Shaw, *Back to Methuselah*, Part 1, Act 1.

Introduction
[1] "The Gospel According to John (Eldredge)", Greg Asimakoupoulos, *Today's Christian*, May/June 2003, www.christianitytoday.com/tc/2003/003/15.10.html.

[2] Robert Harkrider, *Revelation* (Bowling Green: Guardian of Truth Foundation) 223.

Chatper 1: Boot Camp
[1]Theodore Roosevelt, "Citizenship in a Republic." (Speech, Sorbonne, Paris, 23 April 1910).

Chapter 3: A Few Good Men
[1]Henri J.M. Nouwen, *Life of the Beloved* (New York: The Crossroad Publishing Company, 2002), 44.

Chapter 4: The Lord's Infirmary
[1]Arterburn, *Every Man's Battle* (Colorado Springs: Waterbrook Press, 2000), 19–20.

Chapter 5: Selfishness
[1]Vernon K. McLellan, *Wise Words and Quotes* (Wheaton: Tyndale House Publishers, 2000), 56.

[2]King Ferdinand, *Love's Labour's Lost.*

Chapter 6: Sexual Immorality
[1]Consider this report from *The Washington Post:*

Slightly more than half of American teenagers ages 15 to 19 have engaged in oral sex, with females and males reporting similar levels of experience, according to the most comprehensive national survey of sexual behaviors ever released by the federal government. The report...shows that the proportion increases with age to about 70 percent of all 18- and 19-year-olds...

The data also underscore the fact that many young people–particularly those from middle- and upper-income white families–simply do not consider oral sex to be as significant as their parents' generation does...

"The news for parents is that they must broaden the discussions they have with their children about sex and be more specific. If they want their teens to abstain from sex, they need to say exactly what they want their kids to abstain from" (Bill Albert, communications director for the National Campaign to Prevent Teen Pregnancy) (Study: Half Of All Teens Have Had Oral Sex. *Washington Post*; Laura Sessions Stepp; Friday, September 16, 2005).

Chapter 7: Idolatry

[1]John Piper, *Don't Waste Your Life* (Wheaton: Crossway, 2007), 111–112.

For more information on the IMAGE Project, visit

InGodsImage.com

ALSO FROM DEWARD PUBLISHING:

Beneath the Cross:
Essays and Reflections on the Lord's Supper
Jady S. Copeland and Nathan Ward (editors)

The Lord's Supper is rich with meaning supplied by Old Testament foreshadowing and New Testament teaching. Explore the depths of symbolism and meaning found in the last hours of the Lord's life in *Beneath the Cross*. Filled with short essays by preachers, scholars, and other Christians, this book is an excellent tool for preparing meaningful Lord's Supper thoughts—or simply for personal study and meditation. 329 pages. $14.99 (PB); $23.99 (HB).

From Gravel to Glory:
Becoming a House of God
Gina Calvert

Drawing on her studies of the tabernacle and temple, Calvert digs deeply into her own difficult spiritual journey to demonstrate how every experience we have is related to being a house of God. With surprising candor, Calvert takes us from our origins as "a pile of rocks and a promise" to a glorious temple. 185 pages. $12.99.

The Big Picture of the Bible
Kenneth W. Craig

In this short book, the author summarizes the central theme of the Bible in a simple, yet comprehensive approach. Evangelists across the world have used this presentation to convert countless souls to the discipleship of Jesus Christ. Bulk discounts will be available, as will special pricing for congregational orders. 48 pages, color. $4.99.

The Growth of the Seed:
Notes on the Book of Genesis
Nathan Ward

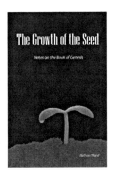

A study of the book of Genesis that emphasizes two primary themes: the development of the Messianic line and the growing enmity between the righteous and the wicked. In addition, it provides detailed comments on the text and short essays on several subjects that are suggested in, yet peripheral to, Genesis. 537 pages. $19.99

The Man of Galilee
Atticus G. Haygood

An apologetic for the deity of Christ using Jesus Himself as presented by the gospel records as its chief evidence. This is a reprint of the 1963 edition. The Man of Galilee was originally published in 1889. 108 pages. $8.99.

Churches of the New Testament
Ethan R. Longhenry

A study designed to investigate every local congregation concerning which the Bible provides some information: it considers the geography and history of each city, whatever is known about the beginnings of the church in the city, and an analysis of the church based upon what is revealed in the New Testament. 150 pages. $9.99.

DE WARD
PUBLISHING COMPANY
dewardpublishing.com

CPSIA information can be obtained at www.ICGtesting.com
Printed in the USA
BVOW030010160113

310657BV00001B/32/P